SAMUEL BECKETT

English Literature

———

Editor

JOHN LAWLOR

Professor of English Language and Literature
in the University of Keele

SAMUEL BECKETT

Francis Doherty

Senior Lecturer in English Language and Literature,
University of Keele

HUTCHINSON UNIVERSITY LIBRARY
LONDON

HUTCHINSON & CO *(Publishers)* LTD

3 Fitzroy Square, London W1

London Melbourne Sydney Auckland
Wellington Johannesburg Cape Town
and agencies throughout the world

First published 1971

*A photograph by Dominic of the National Theatre production
of 'Play' is reproduced on the cover of the paperback edition*

*This book has been set in Fournier type, printed in Great Britain
on smooth wove paper by Anchor Press, and
bound by Wm. Brendon, both of Tiptree, Essex*

ISBN 0 09 109150 0 (cased)
0 09 109151 9 (paper)

FOR MARY

CONTENTS

Foreword   9

Acknowledgements   11

Introduction   13

1 Mind and reality: *Murphy* and *Watt*   25

2 Moribunds in their courses: *Molloy,*
   Malone Dies, The Unnamable   49

3 Theatre of suffering   86

4 Breath-clock breath: *How It Is*   119

5 Farrago of silence and words:
   Short fiction   132

Chronology   148

Bibliography   153

Index   155

FOREWORD

What I have tried to do in this book is to give some indication of the ways that Beckett has taken in fiction and drama, leading from amplitude to compression, from exuberance to tautness; the pursuit of his own special principle of parsimony. I have chosen to do this not by tracing the completeness of the progress towards silence through the whole of his literary output, but have chosen to look closely, if partially, at some of the works which are plotted on that line.

I have tried to take soundings, asking or implying questions about Beckett's treatment of literary form, of the gradual defining of a range of problems and preoccupations in the writing. It seemed the best thing to look as closely as possible at individual works and to raise a number of issues in the discussion of each work which are meant to stimulate the reader into his own exploration of the works, and not to claim any exhausting of the text. Each work of Beckett's is different from its predecessors, though there is a generic relationship, and, because he can make surprising transitions from work to work, I do not wish to reduce the works to a single Beckett landscape.

Very occasionally I give a few words from the French text which we are reading in English, and this is intended partly to suggest second thoughts on Beckett's part, and partly to suggest that it very often repays a reader to compare both the French and the English texts. But, because this work is intended for English readers, quotations are given from the most easily available standard English edition.

One last remark: I have not discussed either Beckett's criticism or his poetry, and this is due partly to considerations of space, but more to the recognition on my part that this is a difficult area to discuss and requires competence greater than that which I possess. But it will become clear to Beckett's readers that the one thing necessary to bear in mind constantly is that this writer is primarily a poet, whatever medium he happens for the moment to be working in, and that his poetry, his imaginative and haunting images, marks a mind unique in our time.

ACKNOWLEDGEMENTS

Acknowledgements are due to the following for the use of copyright material: Calder and Boyars Limited, London, from *Short Stories, Expelled, No's Knife, More Pricks Than Kicks, Murphy, Watt, Molloy, Malone Dies, The Unnameable, How It Is, Texts For Nothing*; and Faber and Faber Limited, London, from *Waiting For Godot, Endgame, All That Fall, Embers, Cascando, Eh Joe*.

Every effort has been made to trace copyright holders and the publishers apologise for any omission.

INTRODUCTION

Samuel Beckett is notoriously elusive as a man, reticent as an author, and nearly completely silent about his own work, so that the literary critic has to piece together what he can about him from fragments. But some of these fragments are helpful to the reader of Beckett's work, aside from one's natural curiosity about the manner of man that this celebrated writer is.

Born into an Irish Protestant, middle-class family in Foxrock, County Dublin, in April 1906, and educated as such, he read Modern Languages (French and Italian) at Trinity College, Dublin. Though academically brilliant, he had time for sports, his favoured being running, cycling and cricket, and we should not think of him ever as totally divorced from the normal world. After his first degree in Trinity in 1927, he spent two years in Paris as English Assistant at the renowned École Normale Supérieure.

Back in Dublin, Beckett had worked on Descartes for a higher degree, but before he did so he used his interest in the life of Descartes to complete a poem for a competition for a poem on Time. He won the £10 prize and *Whoroscope* was published in Paris by the Hours Press in 1930. This poem, though elliptic, sardonic and allusive almost to the point of impenetrability, is useful to the critic as a starting-point for his observations on the continuing use of Descartes by Beckett throughout his career.

At this point Beckett might have seemed to have a promising academic career ahead of him, with a little sideline in creative writing. His first (and only) University post as Assistant to the Professor of Modern Languages at his old College could have been his threshold to great things, and the pleasures of life in a distinguished, ancient and Irish University. But he gave up his post before the academic year was out, saying that he could not presume to teach to others what he did not know himself, and he left Ireland to travel and write. Before he left Dublin he wrote his monograph on Proust, and this was published in London in 1931. This work, though, like much of Beckett's early writing, idiosyncratic and mannered with its cryptic aphoristic style, remains a necessary adjunct for the reader interested in Beckett's theories of fiction. Its statement can be seen to be predictive of Beckett's own concerns, and the discussion of time, memory, love and friendship ought to be a preparation for Beckett's own manipulation of these key concepts. As with the early and continuing place that Descartes has in Beckett's work, one might point to the similar place of Proust and suggest how part of *Krapp's Last Tape* and *How It Is* gains in significance once one remembers Beckett's interest in Proust.

During the years from 1932 to 1936 he wandered in England, France and Germany, and he settled eventually in Paris, no longer to regard Ireland as home. He did visit his mother yearly after the war until her death in 1950, but he does not seem to have been back since. Like all exiles, however, there is possibly a sense in which it could be said that he never left Ireland. Unlike the friend that he came to know and assist in Paris, his fellow Dubliner, James Joyce, his whole output does not draw on Dublin and its environs in the way that Joyce's work from *Stephen Hero* through to *Finnegans Wake* does. Beckett draws on Ireland and his memories of it consistently in his early work from *More Pricks Than Kicks* to *Watt*, which is exclusively written in English, but he continues to draw on his Irishness sporadically, oddly and inconsistently in his later work.

Again, to make a distinction between Beckett and Joyce, two radically contrasted writers: critics like sometimes to talk of Joyce and his unavailing struggle against his Catholicism, and other critics, though with a similar bent, want to see something of this struggle going on in Beckett too. But the facts about Beckett seem very much clearer than those about Joyce, one might suggest. Beckett lost his religious faith early, at least by the time that he entered University, and he remains a man without belief. In a rare interview given to Tom F. Driver from the Union Theological Seminary in New York, he was asked what he thought about those who found a religious significance to his plays. He replied:

Well, really there is none at all. I have no religious feeling. Once I had a religious emotion. It was at my first Communion. No more. My mother was deeply religious. So was my brother. He knelt down at his bed as long as he could kneel. My father had none. The family was Protestant, but for me it was only irksome and I let it go. My brother and mother got no value from their religion when they died. At the moment of crisis it had no more depth than an old-school tie. Irish Catholicism is not attractive, but it is deeper. When you pass a church on an Irish bus, all the hands flurry in the sign of the cross. One day the dogs of Ireland will do that too and perhaps also the pigs. (Tom F. Driver, 'Beckett by the Madeleine', *Columbia University Forum*, Summer, 1961, vol. 4, no. 3, pp. 21–5.)

But if Beckett is to be thus distinguished from Joyce, it would still seem likely that Beckett's years of friendship with Joyce in Paris would have influenced the younger writer. After all, he did help the great artist in the complex reading and copying both of Joyce's manuscript and of arcane works for Joyce's current work, then known as *Work in Progress*, and now as *Finnegans Wake*. Not only did he act as a finder of material that Joyce might be interested in, as copyist and as a friend, but he did translate part of this great work into French—the section known as *Anna Livia Plurabelle*. Beckett's view of all this is very simple: he helped an artist whom he admired by doing odd jobs for him. In response to the question about his 'discipleship' he was firm in another rare interview, this time with the French critic Gabriel d'Aubarède.

——Joyce vous tenait pour un de ses meilleurs traducteurs. Peut-on considérer que vous avez été aussi son disciple? Vos longs monologues intérieurs . . .
——Oh! vous savez, je n'ai traduit personnellement, je veux dire seul, qu' *Anna Livia Plurabel*. Mais j'ai fait des quantités de traductions anonymes, à Paris, pour gagner ma vie.

——Joyce thought of you as one of the best translators of his work. Might one suggest that you were also his disciple? Your long interior monologues . . .
——Oh, well, I only translated personally, I should rather say unassisted, *Anna Livia Plurabelle*. But I have translated lots of work anonymously in Paris in order to live. [My translation]

(*Nouvelles littéraires, artistiques et scientifiques*, 13 February 1961, pp. 1 and 7.)

But there is a simple sense in which Beckett acted as 'disciple', and that is as one of the twelve contributors to the collection of essays which Joyce produced to stimulate interest in *Work in Progress*, for which he had invented the curious title of *Our Examination Round the Factification for Incamination of Work in Progress*. Beckett's essay is one of the highlights of the book, and it interestingly foreshadows his own future work by concentrating on the idea of Purgatory, and by claiming for Joyce's work a perfection where distinctions between form and content can no longer apply. If this is what Beckett learns from Joyce, then he puts into the process more than he takes out, and we should be very wary of making any large claims of indebtedness to Joyce.

As a writer Beckett early shows several characteristics which are now either abandoned or almost refined out of existence, to the regret of some readers. These can be seen in his first large fictional work, *More Pricks Than Kicks*, a collection of stories in the life of the hero, Belacqua Shuah, published in 1934. Its characteristic features are a highly ornate literary style with an obvious love of paraded words, thoroughbreds and high-pacers; a picaresque and involved story-line with its hero victimised by sex and longing for quiet extermination; and a narrator who seems to find joy in the ludicrous sadness of the whole charade. What remains impressive about the book is its ebullience, its love of literary complexities, its parodies, and, above all, its rich comic inventiveness. Looking back on it from our present vantage-point, it carries all its marks of the young man's work, the young academic's work, but it is pulled into the orbit of the later work because it displays at times a compassion seen through an apparent unconcern at the cruelties of existence. The idea of what 'accident' might mean is inspected in the story 'Ding-Dong':

It was a most pleasant street, despite its name, to be abroad in, full as it always was with shabby substance and honest-to-God coming and going. All day the roadway was a tumult of buses, red and blue and silver. By one of these a little girl was run down, just as Belacqua drew near to the railway viaduct. She had been to the Hibernian Dairies for milk and bread and then she had plunged out into the roadway, she was in such a childish fever to get back in record time with her treasure to the tenement in Mark Street where she lived. The good milk was all over the road and the loaf, which had sustained no injury, was sitting up against the kerb, for all the world as though a pair of hands had taken it up and set it down there. The queue standing for the Palace Cinema was torn between conflicting desires: to keep their places and to see the excitement. They craned their necks and called out to know the worst, but they stood firm. Only one girl, debauched in appearance and swathed in a black blanket, fell out near the sting of the queue and secured the loaf. With the loaf under her blanket she sidled unchallenged down Mark Street and turned into Mark Lane. When she got back to the queue her place had been taken of course. But her sally had not cost her more than a couple of yards. (*More Pricks Than Kicks*, p. 43)

As well as this being 'another martyr for old Ireland' because it occurs on Pearse Street (dedicated in memory of this martyred patriot), there seems to be enough of the old-fashioned satirist in this narrator to make us think of him as more than detached and neutral.

The hero of the work is a student of Dante, and bears the name of the slothful Belacqua in Dante's *Divine Comedy* (though one has to grant that the hero's name is constructed on a crude approximation of the low Dublin pronunciation of 'Bollocky Shore'). Dante's Belacqua is to become an ever-receding ambition for the heroes of Beckett's fiction, an ambition of being able to spend eternity re-spending one's life, as Belacqua has to spend his whole life's time over again in Ante-purgatory because he repented of his sins so late in his life. His posture, his resignation and his exclusion from the system are taken up again and again in Beckett.

> Among them one,
> Who seem'd to be much wearied, sat him down,
> And with his arms did fold his knees about,
> Holding his face between them downward bent. . . .
>
> 'Behoves so long that heaven first bear me round
> Without its limits, as in life it bore;
> Because I, to the end, repentant sighs
> Delay'd; if prayer do not aid me first,
> That riseth up from heart which lives in grace.
> What other kind avails, not heard in heaven?'

('Purgatory', Canto IV, ll. 102–3; 188–93. *The Vision: or Hell, Purgatory, and Paradise of Dante Alighieri*, trans. by the Rev. Henry Francis Cary.)[1]

Perhaps a footnote which Cary gives is equally to be remembered. He quotes a note written in Latin in the Monte Casino Manuscript: 'This Belacqua was an excellent master of the harp and lute, but very negligent in his affairs both spiritual and temporal.' This is useful to the reader of Beckett because Belacqua Shuah is the first of several figures in Beckett who are accomplished artists and yet 'very negligent in their

1. 1898 edition, pp. 196–7. First published in London in 1814.

affairs both spiritual and temporal', figures whose ability to confront
or organise reality is deficient (to say the very least). He is the proto-
type of the hero who dreams of absolution from life, poised between
modes of being, and he is the first in that chain which runs from this
dream into the nightmare of the later fiction.

The next hero in Beckett's fiction is Murphy in the novel *Murphy*,
published in 1938, and in its time attracting little critical comment.
James Joyce thought well enough of it and its author to make amends
for a limerick he made on it which began with 'There was a young man
named Murphy' by quoting from memory a passage from Murphy's
will with its instructions for his last resting-place. It has been seen as
having influenced Iris Murdoch, and it was admired by Dylan
Thomas and some others of rare discernment.

Though Murphy seems to share no concern with his predecessor for
the work of Dante, he does share some things with him. He is a victim
of life, though he is given an escape-route into his mind away from the
'buzzing confusion' of reality, and he seems to leave this life in a way
which reminds the reader of Belacqua's exit. The earlier hero had been
bungled out of life by medical incompetence while under an anaesthetic
for the removal of an anthrax from his neck:

> He bounced up on to the table like a bridegroom. The local doc was in great
> form, he had just come from standing best man, he was all togged up under
> his vestments. He recited his exhortation and clapped on the nozzle.
>   'Are you right?' said Belacqua.
> The mixture was too rich, there could be no question about that. His heart
> was running away, terrible yellow yerks in his skull. 'One of the best,' he
> heard those words that did not refer to him. The expression reassured him.
> The best man clawed at his tap.
>   By Christ! he did die!
>   They had clean forgotten to auscultate him!
>
> (*More Pricks Than Kicks*, p. 186)

Murphy departs while he has retreated from his body into his mind and
someone inadvertently pulls the wrong chain in the lavatory below his
garret, filling the garret with gas which explodes, taking Murphy with
it. Murphy is rocking in his rocking chair:

> Slowly he felt better, astir in his mind, in the freedom of that light and dark
> that did not clash, nor alternate, nor fade nor lighten except to their com-
> munion. The rock got faster and faster, shorter and shorter, the gleam was
> gone, the grin was gone, the starlessness was gone, soon his body would be

quiet. Most things under the moon got slower and slower and then stopped, a rock got faster and faster and then stopped. Soon his body would be quiet, soon he would be free.

The gas went on in the w.c., excellent gas, superfine chaos. Soon his body was quiet. (*Murphy*, pp. 172–3)

Things are managed more finely in *Murphy*, and the kinds of doubt about events, which one comes to recognise more clearly as the mature Beckett's hallmark, begin to creep in. Murphy leaves a will (most unexpectedly) and has very definite ideas of the future resting-place of his remains. There are other clues which might lead one to suspect that this is a planned suicide, timed to take place during self-annihilation during meditation, but we never have certainty one way or another.

Murphy, too, is rich in comic invention, is highly amusing, and more restrictive in its use of recondite words and expressions, and is a self-proclaimed parody of the form of the novel. But the isolation of the central character is clearer than that of his predecessor, and his concern with the mind and its privacy more insistent and cogent.

At the outbreak of the war in 1939 Beckett was in Ireland, but, preferring France in war to Ireland in peace, as he said, he returned to Paris. A little while later he became involved with the French Resistance and only escaped the Gestapo by ten minutes. He left Paris and spent the rest of the war living out the role of a French peasant in the Vaucluse near Avignon. In the short time he had spent in Paris he had worked on a translation of *Murphy* into French, and through the war years he wrote his last novel in English, *Watt*, which remained unpublished until well after the war, in 1953.

Watt not only represents the end of Beckett's English fiction, but is the first of the long series of works which confront squarely the possibility of man's discovering meaning in life. It answers the question 'What?' by 'Not!' as Watt, for unknowable reasons, enters the service of Mr Knott. The novel is filled with puzzles, insoluble problems and exhaustive lists of the possible combinations of factors in any situation, and there is a troubling manipulation of the conventions of novel-writing, meant to make the reader less and less secure in any kind of certainty that he might have about the novel.

Where the earlier novel, *Murphy*, had mockingly presented a world in pursuit of a non-heroic hero whose concern is a solipsistic self-communion, this novel shows painfully the tragic comedy of a mind breaking in the process of its pursuit of meaning. The early wry comedy of *Murphy* gives place to a metaphysical farce of cruelty taking place in the midst of an unconcerned and smugly self-satisfied Irish world which can proclaim on its penultimate page that 'Life isn't such a bad old bugger' (*Watt*, John Calder, 1963, p. 245).

After the war, from 1945 to 1950, Beckett had a creative surge, writing in French, his adopted language, and living for his writing, rarely moving out of his flat in Paris. Aside from the publication of his French translation of *Murphy* in 1947, Beckett seemed to be silent, but he was producing his trilogy of novels, *Molloy, Malone Meurt,* and *L'Innommable,* the *Nouvelles* and *Textes pour Rien,* and his most successful play *En Attendant Godot.* Two further works belong to this period, a play *Eleutheria,* unpublished, but written in 1947 and read by a few favoured critics in manuscript, and a novel, *Mercier et Camier,* unpublished until 1970.

In the trilogy of novels, *Molloy, Malone Dies* and *The Unnamable* (to give their English titles), Beckett traces the search for self, the hunt for identity by writers through writing. By choosing characters who all try to pursue a meaning for their existence, and who can be seen in progressive states of decay and asylum from the ordinary world, Beckett more and more closely approaches the problem of the writer who uses writing in order to avoid the inevitable task of facing himself. But facing oneself, if one's existence is only that of a writer of stories, will become increasingly impossible when all the stories are taken away. It is as though Beckett were rebuking himself for the writing of *Watt* (and all the previous fiction) as a way of pushing his own problems away from himself and into *Watt.*

The trilogy is a gradual approach towards the problems of the nature of the self, the nature of language and the nature of creation. All provisional answers must be discarded; all provisional foundations must be dismantled; and the generously deceptive flamboyance of Beckett's natural English style must be replaced by the more astringent French. But one might note that somehow Beckett's Irishness remains. The characters retain their Irish names, move in a landscape compounded of France and Ireland, and measure in feet and inches, and use shillings for money.

The path of Beckett's fiction since the writing of *The Unnamable* has been one of some difficulty. He turned back to the short form of the story as a possible way out of his fictional dilemmas after his writing of

Watt, and he turned to a connected series of short pieces of writing, the *Textes pour Rien*, after writing *L'Innommable*.

After these experiments with fiction, both the trilogy, the *Nouvelles* and the *Textes pour Rien*, the later fiction of Beckett has become more and more compressed, discarding more and more, reducing all fictional elements to an almost incredible sparseness. But the more concentrated and denuded the style, and the shorter the piece, the more it approaches a non-novel existence as a complexly working poem. The sparer the technique, it would seem, the more resonant the 'fiction', and Beckett has the power to create hauntingly powerful images and clusters of words which comment sadly and painfully on many images which we have inherited from our past Western European culture. The tautness of the latest short fictions is a unique yet characteristic achievement, and the ringing power of desolation which comes to the reader of *Imagination Dead Imagine* (1965) or the hearer of *Lessness* (first broadcast by the BBC in February 1971) is undeniable.

Beckett's career as a dramatist begins with the publication of *En Attendant Godot* in 1952, and this play remains as the one by which he is known to a wide audience. It has caused a great deal of critical ink to be spent, and its impact on the theatre has been very great indeed, largely because it raises some very fundamental questions about the nature of a play and what it can jettison and still remain a play. It continues to offer a bleak world of empty hopes, coagulated culture, and a fragmented world running down into infinity for the audiences who continue to witness it throughout the world. It offers an uncomfortable comedy of desolation, and the meaning of the play must continue to remain elusive. This makes for more discomfort, but we have grown to know very well the homeless wanderers who are living in the impossible hope that Godot will come tomorrow. These are the human representatives that Beckett allows us, and the play is perhaps best seen as a parable of life, but a parable which allows each interpreter of it room for his own interpretation, while sanctioning no single interpretation.

When Beckett had finished this drama with its logically interminable world, he turned the attention of his newly found readership to the fiction which followed the play, and this audience then discovered the works which had preceded it. Then, five years after the appearance of *En Attendant Godot*, he published *Fin de Partie* in 1957, to be translated and issued in English the following year as *Endgame*. From the bleak expanse of an empty road to nowhere of the previous play, and from the contrasting worlds of the static figures of Vladimir and Estragon and the dynamically retarding Pozzo and Lucky, this play moves inside and into the last abode. Instead of *Waiting for Godot* and its endlessly unending end, we are here waiting for the end: 'Finished, it's finished, nearly finished, it must be nearly finished'. But this play cannot finish either, and we are made aware of the growing disintegration, the gradual denuding of the features of this world, without any merciful final termination for it all. There is less action in this play, though *acting* takes its place, and the audience is made painfully aware that it *is* an *audience* of a play that insists that it is all a *play*, all a series of meaningless dramatic games. Yet it is a moving play, because it seems to set before us a common enough fear and feeling that we invent the meaning for our world in the face of evident decay and deliquescence.

Beckett's work in the theatre shows the same overall pattern as the rest of his later work: it calls in question the nature of the medium it is working with (in this case accepted ideas of a play) and then follows a path of reduction and diminution. The scale runs from two-act plays, like *Waiting for Godot* and the smaller, two-character drama *Happy Days* of 1961, down into one-act plays which grow smaller and smaller, with less and less action, until one reaches the latest 'dramaticule', *Breath*. There we have no protagonist, no action, no words; a heap of junk fills the centre of the stage, light dims and comes up again, and a recording fills the auditorium with the sound of a breath inhaled, held, exhaled, and a birth-death cry terminates and initiates this endless 'action', which, though repeated four times, ought to follow its path into the infinity of man's simple continuing of this pattern of 'life'.

His dramatic media include radio and television (and a single film, *Film*, with Buster Keaton in the main role), and his excursions into these media have shown one remarkable quality. He has tried to examine and comprehend the peculiar properties of each medium, and then to turn the medium into his vision, not translating his special vision crudely into a new medium. This fact gives his pieces for radio a special interest, and his television play, *Eh Joe*, is an almost unique example of a dramatist's turning the camera into real account in the play.

But whatever medium of drama Beckett has worked in, the resulting creation has that characteristic density, spareness and desolation which one comes to associate with all his work. The career of his writing has gradually reduced the magniloquence and amplitude of a learned wit, the sardonic and macabre inheritor of a tradition of savage humour, the aider and friend of jocoserious Joyce, into silence, or, more accurately, wordlessness.

I

MIND AND REALITY:

Murphy and *Watt*

Beckett's early novels show his emergence from a ludicrous and mocking world, of a world in pursuit of a non-heroic hero whose concern is a solipsistic self-communion into a world where the mind searches for a meaning and breaks in the process. The early wry comedy of *Murphy* gives place to a metaphysical farce of cruelty taking place in the midst of an unconcerned and smugly self-satisfied world which can proclaim that 'Life isn't such a bad old bugger'.

Murphy

Beckett's first novel to be published appeared in 1938 and excited few people, though memories are racing to bring out those of rare perception (the older James Joyce reciting part admiringly to his young friend Beckett, the young Oxford don reading passages to an admiring audience). Its central figure has no Christian name known to us, and will be the first of such heroes in Beckett's fiction, but he is Irish and the book he appears in is flamboyantly so. The story, such as it is, deals with the search for Murphy and Murphy's search contemporaneously for annihilation. The plot crosses love for Murphy and Murphy's self-love, *Amor intellectualis quo Murphy se ipsum amat*, in a complex little system of loss and gain, which can be stigmatised, as in the novel, by the horse-leech's daughter (Proverbs, xxx. 15, 'The leech has daughters twain: "Give, give!" is their refrain'). A chain of need for love extends from Murphy and binds two women to him, Celia Kelly, a prostitute in London who picks him up and who loves him, and Miss

Counihan from Cork who loves him, provided that Murphy is seeking his fortune in London. The chain of love extends back from Miss Counihan to Neary, Murphy's philosophic mentor, and Wylie, a former fellow pupil of Murphy, who in this nexus both love Miss Counihan.

Beckett seems to have two concerns in *Murphy*; the one to attempt a story novel in third-person narration which will be parodic at as many points as possible of the average novel's plot, method of narration, characterisation, conversation and authorial power. The other, to write as excitingly, as amusingly and as unusually as his style, vocabulary, learning and rhetoric will permit. Nothing is simple, and all has been trampled over by fiction-writers for so long that what Beckett needs to do, one feels, is to mock the mode and yet remain within it, because no way yet exists of writing in an entirely new mode. What seems to control his interest is not really the attempt to delineate an interesting state of mind such as Murphy might be claimed to have, which can occupy itself with itself to the exclusion of the body, nor to write a kind of metaphysical parable, but to write within an established novel tradition, and to invest everything, where possible, with an amused but sardonic intellectual venom. The same energy and pleasure can construct devastating and attacking sentences and lyrically effusive and beautifully cadenced prose. Entirely typical of the energy and the lyrical impulse salted with cunning undercutting might be the presentation of the three Irish Murphy-hunters on p. 83:

He sat on, shaking his head like a perhaps empty bottle, muttering bitterly with the chop-sticks, and a sorer lack than any wife or even mistress, were she Yang Kuei-fei herself, was a mind to pillow his beside. The Oriental milieu had no doubt to do with this aberration. The ly-chee, of which he had taken three portions, continued to elaborate its nameless redolence, a dusk of lute music behind his troubles.

Miss Counihan sat on Wylie's knee, *not* in Wynn's Hotel lest an action for libel should lie, and oyster kisses passed between them. Wylie did not often kiss, but when he did it was a serious matter. He was not one of those lugubrious persons who insist on removing the clapper from the bell of passion. A kiss from Wylie was like a breve tied, in a long slow amorous phrase, over bars' times its equivalent in demi-semiquavers. Miss Counihan had never enjoyed anything quite so much as this slow-motion osmosis of love's spittle.

This is what everyone would recognise as *written*, as so fully inventive that the context of the novel is not simply that of bravura writing in general, but of the contest of skill in wit and extravagance. Its Dublin origins seem to be unmistakable in this, as they are in the delighted mocking of institutions, persons and things sacred to the Irish. The sentimental urge to commemorate Easter Week 1916 with the erection of a statue of Cuchulain in the General Post Office in O'Connell Street is obviously rebuked by the delightful extravagance of the opening of chapter 4:

In Dublin a week later, that would be September 19th, Neary minus his whiskers was recognised by a former pupil called Wylie, in the General Post Office, contemplating from behind the statue of Cuchulain. Neary had bared his head, as though the holy ground meant something to him. Suddenly he flung aside his hat, sprang forward, seized the dying hero by the thighs and began to dash his head against his buttocks, such as they are. The Civic Guard on duty in the building, roused from a tender reverie by the sound of blows, took in the situation at his leisure, disentangled his baton and advanced with measured tread, thinking he had caught a vandal in the act. Happily Wylie, whose reactions as a street bookmaker's stand were as rapid as a zebra's, had already seized Neary round the waist, torn him back from the sacrifice and smuggled him half-way to the exit.

A mind set on the delights of oblique, satiric and heavily allusive statement puts a premium on the manner of performance and rejoices in as many kinds of comedy as can be engineered. Ludovic Janvier sees, quite properly, the burlesque seriousness of *Murphy* when he says, 'il sagit de la course-poursuite d'Andromaque jouée par les Marx Brothers' (*Pour Samuel Beckett*, p. 27). 'Andromaque played by the Marx Brothers' is good, but the comedy leaves Murphy relatively untouched. It happens around him not with him, and his story is one of a closing of the bodily life and activities of Murphy. He parodies intellectual life, still bearing with him the fragments of his life as an amateur theological student, even to the clothing of an aeruginous black suit:

One beheld in fact a relic of those sanguine days when as a theological student he had used to lie awake night after night with Bishop Bouvier's *Supplementum ad Tractatum de Matrimonio* under his pillow. (p. 52)

He has by now become 'a strict non-reader' (p. 113) and can be called a 'seedy solipsist' (p. 59) whose dream is the 'Belacqua fantasy', and who has a method of 'being laid asleep in his body to become a living mind' (to parody Wordsworth) by rocking naked and bound in his rocking-chair. But even this can be superior to the 'Belacqua fantasy' which is fully exposed on pp. 56–7.

At this moment Murphy would willingly have waived his expectation of Antepurgatory for five minutes in his chair, renounced the lee of Belacqua's rock and his embryonal repose, looking down at dawn across the reeds to the trembling of the austral sea and the sun obliquing to the north as it rose, immune from expiation until he should have dreamed it all through again, with the downright dreaming of an infant, from the spermarium to the crematorium. He thought so highly of this post-mortem situation, its advantages were present in such detail to his mind, that he actually hoped he might live to be old. Then he would have a long time lying there dreaming, watching the dayspring run through its zodiac, before the toil up hill to Paradise. The gradient was outrageous, one in less than one. God grant no godly chandler would shorten his time with a good prayer.

This was his Belacqua fantasy and perhaps the most highly systematized of the whole collection. It belonged to those that lay just beyond the frontiers of suffering, it was the first landscape of freedom.

He is the object of derision from most of the world which witnesses the strange apparition, though those who think they know him best need him for their own reasons—none of which seem to be concerned with Murphy but with a Murphy-mirror of their own needs. The one exception to all of this is Celia, the heavenly, the good professional prostitute whom Murphy deserts and for whom Murphy has an unfortunate love, unfortunate in the sense that it, like his predilection for ginger biscuits over others, prevents his total abnegation of this 'muckball' of an earth. Murphy's search for abnegation, for ablation, is conducted by the author (but, we are led to believe, by a chain of happy accidents) to the final happy accident of his combustion in his attic, gas-filled by someone pulling the wrong chain in the lavatory below. He has no 'character' but is seen as a mind, burdened by the material, by the cognitive and emotional lumber of a life, on its way to itself by jettisoning as quickly as possible all its habiliments, snares and encumbrances. He casts off his clothes one by one and tries to picture some person from his past.

He could not get a picture in his mind of any creature he had met, animal or human, scraps of bodies, of landscapes, hands, eyes, lines and colours evoking nothing, rose and climbed out of sight before him, as though reeled upward off a spool level with his throat. (p. 172)

He is not going to commit suicide, nor to escape the body in a final successful leap, but is dimly aware of a determination to return to Celia. The author's accidents take over and he is burnt to death, one assumes, in a state of mind-absorbed self-awareness, with the body 'quiet'.

On his progress to this fitting extinction Murphy moves from a world of trivia and trivial occupations made pretentious by people's talk and people's needs, of the universally valid classification of experience into

jokes that had once been good jokes and jokes that had never been good jokes. What but an imperfect sense of humour could have made such a mess of chaos. And so on. (p. 48)

And the joke is on Murphy when he leaves via the gas-route:

The gas went on in the w.c., excellent gas, superfine chaos. (p. 173)

It is Chaos because Murphy decides (rightly) that etymologically 'gas' is the same as 'chaos'.

And the etymology of gas? Could it be the same word as chaos? Hardly. Chaos was yawn. But then cretin was Christian. Chaos would do, it might not be right but it was pleasant, for him henceforward gas would be chaos, and chaos gas. It could make you yawn, warm, laugh, cry, cease to suffer, live a little longer, die a little sooner. What could it not do? Gas. Could it turn a neurotic into a psychotic? No. Only God could do that. Let there be Heaven in the midst of the waters, let it divide the waters. The Chaos and Waters Facilities Act. The Chaos, Light and Coke Co. Hell. Heaven. Helen. Celia. (p. 121–2)

Murphy's death is therefore expected, and, when it comes, it is a version of 'take into the air my quiet breath' with a rich tissue of ironic cross-fertilising reference. He finds his ideal home which will be the entrance to his long-home in a genuine garret, long sought and only known once before 'in the first cyanosis of youth' when

Murphy had occupied a garret in Hanover, not for long, but for long enough to experience all its advantages. Since then he had sought high and low for another, even half as good. In vain. What passed for a garret in Great Britain and Ireland was really nothing more than an attic. An attic! How was it possible for such a confusion to arise? A basement was better than an attic. An attic!

But the garret that he now saw was not an attic, nor yet a mansard, but a genuine garret, not half, but twice as good as the one in Hanover, because half as large. (p. 113)

He finds a better garret than the one in Hanover, and Ludovic Janvier reminds us of Leibniz in Hanover (op. cit., p. 27) and the monad that Murphy is to become, as we later recognise the poor approximation of the garret to the padded cells in the Magdalen Mercy Seat. In summarising the beauties of the 'pads' we are led to statements such as that

No system of ventilation appeared to dispel the illusion of responsible vacuum. The compartment was windowless, like a monad, except for the shuttered judas in the door, at which a sane eye appeared, or was employed to appear, at frequent and regular intervals throughout the twenty-four hours. (p. 125)

The self-exclusiveness of the monad and the self-inclusiveness of Murphy's mind, to which section six of the book is devoted (*Amor intellectualis quo Murphy se ipsum amat*), are directly related to Mr Endon, Murphy's favourite patient at the M.M.M., Endon being Greek for 'within', and his condition of 'a schizophrenic of the most amiable variety' meant that he had, as a 'higher schizoid', escaped into his little world completely. This meant that Murphy could witness and approach a successful example of those whose minds were places and not instruments, a model for his ideal, because Murphy

whose experience as a physical and rational being obliged him to call sanctuary what the psychiatrists called exile and to think of the patients not as banished from a system of benefits but as escaped from a colossal fiasco. (p. 123)

Accordingly, when they play chess together it is to play chess in such a way that no one wins a piece, that no one wins. The idea of chess is of war, of assault and defence against an enemy, an opponent, but to play without regard for the idea of an opponent, only to move all the pieces out and back again to their original positions would be an ideal treatment of others, present, perhaps necessary, but among whom one moves independently, aloof and alone. Murphy only gradually comes to recognise the complete independence of Mr Endon, because Murphy still retains his humanity. Playing at first with Mr Endon so that 'sometimes, after eight or nine hours of this guerilla, neither player would have lost a piece or even checked the other', Murphy feels this as

an expression of kinship with Mr Endon and made him if possible more chary of launching an attack than by nature he was. (p. 129)

But, we are told, Mr Endon sees nothing of kinship in Murphy when later Murphy, on his second round of the cells on his one and only night duty, sees Mr Endon sitting on the head of his bed with the chess game set up on it.

Murphy resumed his round, gratified in no small measure. Mr Endon had recognised the feel of his friend's eye upon him and made his preparations accordingly. Friend's eye? Say rather, Murphy's eye. Mr Endon had felt

Murphy's eye upon him. Mr Endon would have been less than Mr Endon if he had known what it was to have a friend; and Murphy more than Murphy if he had not hoped against his better judgment that his feeling for Mr Endon was in some small degree reciprocated. Whereas the sad truth was, that while Mr Endon for Murphy was no less than bliss, Murphy for Mr Endon was no more than chess. Murphy's eye? Say rather, the chessy eye. Mr Endon had vibrated to the chessy eye upon him and made his preparations accordingly. (p. 164)

Then playing the astounding non-game, with Mr Endon's last piece neatly back on its official position (43. Q – Q 1), White (Murphy) surrenders and Murphy passes into Nothing, the absence (to abuse a nice distinction) not of *percipere* but of *percipi* (p. 168). On returning the escaped Endon back to his cell, Murphy sees that he is not seen by Mr Endon, however close he comes to the eyes, however carefully and beautifully observed in all their curious detail, 'seeing himself stigmatised in those eyes that did not see him' (pp. 170–1). Murphy hears words which he has to speak, and we hear four versions of the idea of the unseeing seen and the seeing unseen:

> 'the last at last seen of him
> himself unseen by him
> and of himself'.

From there 'to the infinite riches in a w.c.' is a short step across the long grass towards the male nurses' quarters and extinction, return by gas/chaos whence he came. If an accident in the lavatory leads to death, Murphy had already determined to set ironies richly together by his last request found singed in an envelope addressed to Mrs Murphy 'and the address in Brewery Road, pencilled in laborious capitals':

With regard to the disposal of these my body, mind and soul, I desire that they be burnt and placed in a paper bag and brought to the Abbey Theatre, Lr. Abbey Street, Dublin, and without pause into what the great and good Lord Chesterfield calls the necessary house, where their happiest hours have been spent, on the right as one goes down into the pit, and I desire that the chain be there pulled upon them, if possible during the performance of a piece, the whole to be executed without ceremony or show of grief. (p. 183)

But the infinity of ironic guffaw is strictly curtailed by the elaborate care with which Beckett ensures that Murphy's residual ashes stay where they belong:

Some hours later Cooper took the packet of ash from his pocket, where earlier in the evening he had put it for greater security, and threw it angrily

B

at a man who had given him great offence. It bounced, burst, off the wall on to the floor, where at once it became the object of much dribbling, passing, trapping, shooting, punching, heading and even some recognition from the gentleman's code. By closing time the body, mind and soul of Murphy were freely distributed over the floor of the saloon; and before another dayspring greyened the earth had been swept away with the sand, the beer, the butts, the glass, the matches, the spits, the vomit. (p. 187)

The saddened comedy of man's ending, no matter how small his designs, the subjugation of ambitions, however narrowed and however gratified, to the way of the world, to accidents, to the dung-heap, takes over from the metaphysical search for self-sufficiency *Murphy* had been concerned with. The novel's people are the doodles of a gifted stylistic comedian with a bent for the unusual, for Steiss's nosonomy, for rhetorical extravagance ('that long hank of Apollonian asthenia', groaned Neary, 'that schizoidal spasmophile . . .'), and for outrageous puns (but no more outrageous than God's) like Miss Carridge. Here in *Murphy* is Beckett's plenty and later works will refine aspects of the novel, paring away and selecting more and more ruthlessly.

Whatever one might think about Murphy as a central figure for a novel, he has a collection of attributes and we can see his eccentricities and be amused by them, not puzzled. We accept, for instance, the grotesque comedy of the fiasco with the five biscuits and the verbal pratfall, followed by the indecent assaults on his biscuits spread out on the grass by the Dachshund while Murphy had been too absorbed in the 'touching little argonautic' of the lady vainly tempting sheep with lettuce. The comedy of the vainly speculative man confronted and beaten by the inrush of external events will give way to man's recognition of the beautiful absurdity, the inhuman clarity of computation. In *Murphy* the comic extravagance of the language betrays the mocker; in later works the joke will be against the reader. So, in *Murphy*, we have the problem of overcoming prejudice for or against a particular biscuit:

Even if he conquered his prejudice against the anonymous, still there would be only twenty-four ways in which the biscuits could be eaten. But were he to take the final step and overcome his infatuation with the ginger, then the assortment would spring to life before him, dancing the radiant measure of its total permutability, edible in a hundred and twenty ways! (p. 68)

Murphy is, of course, in process of renunciation, following his own *via negativa*, and there remains a serious point here, but one feels that

Beckett needs to complicate the telling, to overinflate the language (not that it's not funny—it is). But, for example, in *Molloy*, computation works at mocking the reader as well as the mind that puts its trust in it.

And in winter, under my greatcoat, I wrapped myself in swathes of news-paper, and did not shed them until the earth awoke, for good, in April. The *Times Literary Supplement* was admirably adapted to this purpose, of a never failing toughness and impermeability. Even farts made no impression on it. I can't help it, gas escapes from my fundament on the least pretext, it's hard not to mention it now and then, however great my distaste. One day I counted them. Three hundred and fifteen farts in nineteen hours, or an average of over sixteen farts an hour. After all it's not excessive. Four farts every fifteen minutes. It's nothing. Not even one fart every four minutes. It's unbelievable. Damn it, I hardly fart at all. I should never have mentioned it. Extraordinary how mathematics help you to know yourself. (p. 30)

Murphy is the only one of Beckett's characters who is allowed to die during the work, though his death is both absurd and yet by special dispensation of accidents controlled by the omnipotent author, the only character in the novel who is not called a puppet by his creator ('All the puppets in this book whinge sooner or later, except Murphy, who is not a puppet', p. 86). After Murphy, all the Ms and inverted Ms (Ws) will have their several journeys to make but without hope of crucifixion on this increasingly intolerable *via dolorosa*.

The one person from the curious assemblage of grotesques who people the novel who will not appear again with her selflessness, love and generous humanity is Celia, and, as she is unique, a word is in place. Put against Miss Carridge or Miss Counihan she shines like a beautiful and innocent child, and seen in the context of impossibles like Cooper, she is human. Cooper one remembers as existing on the far extreme of the spectrum of the parodic human in the book:

Cooper's only visible human characteristic was a morbid craving for alco-holic depressant. So long as he could be kept off the bottle he was an in-valuable servant. He was a low-sized, clean-shaven, grey-faced, one-eyed man, triorchous and a non-smoker. He had a curious limited walk, like that of a destitute diabetic in a strange city. He never sat down and never took off his hat. (p. 41)

The novel ends with Celia pushing her grandfather, another absurdity clinging to life, slowly against the elements into a future which is bleak but home. She has had to go back on the streets to support herself since Murphy's death, though her success is now strictly limited. Today she has caught the attentions of 'a week-end lecher well advanced in years,

sprawling on his sacrum (which was a mass of eczema)', and yesterday
'a kid and a drunk'. A bad business doing bad business. This is intended, one feels, as a real gesture of sympathy and absolution towards
Celia, but the final lines of the novel show courage and doggedness
against the necessities, and there's no way out in a comic or a grotesque
death for her.

Celia toiled along the narrow path into the teeth of the wind, then faced north
up the wide hill. There was no shorter way home. The yellow hair fell across
her face. The yachting-cap clung like a clam to the skull. The levers were the
tired heart. She closed her eyes.
   'All out.'

Watt

After *Murphy*'s appearance before the war Beckett was silent. But,
during those years of war, in hiding from the Germans because of his
involvement with the Resistance and playing the part of a French
peasant in the Vaucluse, his ideas on Fiction altered. The product of
those years, *Watt*, is his last full novel to be written in English, and,
though only published in 1953 in France and in 1959 in England, was
completed by 1945.

   This novel is perhaps the most difficult of Beckett's because it is an
obvious transition from the kind of novel that *Murphy* represents to
the later fiction. The opening, which has no connection with the novel
proper, presents parodic Dubliners who are engaged in the novelists'
game of narrowing a group of people to a common focus, a united concern with the central character. The technique of minor characters
meeting 'accidentally' and becoming aware of the central figure's importance in their lives is grotesquely parodied. The events themselves
are really self-enclosed, a closed world of petty concerns, love,
marriage, the family, the outsider, crime of passion, love lost and won.
Here the jolly Beckett has a final flowering. Love is absurd, comic:

For the lady held the gentleman by the ears, and the gentleman's hand was
on the lady's thigh, and the lady's tongue was in the gentleman's mouth.
Tired of waiting for the train, said[1] Mr Hackett, they strike up an acquain-
tance. (p. 6)
   1. Much valuable space has been saved, in this work, that would otherwise have been
lost, by avoidance of the plethoric reflexive pronoun after *say*.

The pedantry of the interrupting authorial note is Sternean, deliberately insisting on a formal author-reader relationship, the claim being

made and met that someone is in control, someone is telling the tale. The characters are made to dance in a portrayal of bathetic concerns, shot with irony and parody. Mrs Nixon's child Larry is an inversion of the Larry of song: 'The night before Larry was stretched':

> You remember the night that Larry was born, said the lady.
> I do, said the gentleman.
> How old is Larry now? said Mr Hackett.
> How old is Larry, my dear? said the gentleman.
> How old is Larry, said the lady. Larry will be forty years old next March, D.V.
> That is the kind of thing Dee always vees, said Mr Hackett.
> I wouldn't go as far as that, said the gentleman. (p. 10)

Into this comedy of ill-manners Watt is deposited from a passing tram,

> a solitary figure, lit less and less by the receding lights, until it was scarcely to be distinguished from the dim wall behind it. Tetty was not sure whether it was a man or a woman. Mr Hackett was not sure that it was not a parcel, a carpet for example, or a roll of tarpaulin, wrapped up in dark paper and tied about the middle with a cord. (p. 14)

So, Watt is mysterious and arouses just the right sort of interest and concern in the characters, just right, that is, for a parody of the expected novelists' procedures. Mr Hackett

> did not know when he had been more intrigued, nay, he did not know when he had been so intrigued. He did not know either what it was that so intrigued him. What is it that so intrigues me, he said, whom even the extraordinary, even the supernatural, intrigue so seldom, and so little. Here there is nothing in the least unusual, that I can see, and yet I burn with curiosity, and with wonder. (p. 15)

What remains of excess, of inflated rhetorical introduction to the eponymous hero, is necessarily deflated, retracted, expunged.

> The sensation is not disagreeable, I must say, and yet I do not think I could bear it for more than twenty minutes, or half an hour. (ibid.)

What might have happened to Mr Hackett's interest is faintly shadowed just a little later: he might have been coupled with Watt in one of those pseudo-couples like Mercier and Camier, Molloy and Moran, but that remains for other novels. All we have here is Mr Nixon's observations to Mr Hackett:

> The curious thing is, my dear fellow, I tell you quite frankly, that when I see him, or think of him, I think of you, and that when I see you, or think of you, I think of him. I have no idea why this is so. (pp. 16–17)

Neither do we, but we have the unexplored possibility, as we have the repeated questions from Mr Hackett to Mr Nixon about Watt, of whom little is known, and that little perplexing. Yet Mr Hackett feels himself into Watt's situation and hypothesises beautifully, doing the novelist's job of presenting information about a character through sympathetic understanding of other characters. Yet nothing is to be trusted by the reader, as Watt is an enigma—a what? The day goes down, Mr and Mrs Nixon withdraw, and Mr Hackett is left scratching his hump in the dark:

Yes, now the western sky was as the eastern, which was as the southern, which was as the northern. (p. 22)

And that *Dubliners* world is left in a closed formality of an ending only to open into the confusion of Watt's world, of incompetence among objects, of haphazardy and falling. The station platform with its porter wheeling milk-churns full and empty in a parody of a punishment task (to be taken up again in *The Unnamable*) and its departing newsagent give Beckett enough material for a beautiful display of descriptive writing, presenting a narrowed world in incisive detail, writing a leisurely and careful prose that rings out the last of the well-known world where the absurdity of details of a man's walk, behaviour and clothing are lovingly noted for their own sakes, where they are not expected to have meaning other than that of pretending that people *are* their occupation (newsagent), their recreation (to 'play a game of chess, between masters, out of Mr Staunton's handbook'), their clothing ('But one thought of him as the man who, among other things, never left off his cap, a plain blue cloth cap, with a peak and a knob'), their gait ('He was short and limped dreadfully. When he got started he moved rapidly, in a series of aborted genuflexions').

As the train gets under way towards a destination withheld from the reader, the last candidate for our attention before Watt's entrance into Mr Knott's household is a Mr Dum Spiro (*Dum Spiro Spero*: While I breathe I hope), the editor of *Crux*, 'the popular catholic monthly.' He presents the theological old world, with its own fascinating absurdities soluble by anyone with leisure to become familiar with the lists of theological conundrum solvers.

A rat, or other small animal, eats of a consecrated wafer
1. Does he ingest the Real Body, or does he not?
2. If he does not, what has become of it?

3. If he does, what is to be done with him?
Mr Spiro now replied to these questions, that is to say he replied to question one and he replied to question three. He did so at length, quoting from Saint Bonaventura, Peter Lombard, Alexander of Hales, Sanchez, Suarez, Henno, Diana, Concina and Dens, for he was a man of leisure. (pp. 26–7)

From these metaphysical speculators we move into another world equally metaphysical, and equally full of conundrums, and flooded with a theological reference of an anti-theological importance. Watt is entering a world with nothing at its centre, not a mystic's world with its search for and yearning towards the central luminous significance of Being, of that union of Being and Existence Christians call God, but a mystic's world of abnegation, of obliteration of self in order to come closer and into a union with Nothing. Arsene, whose valedictory speech is Watt's formal introduction into the world where words slip and fail, where significance is altered or random or more meaningful than in the normal Mr Hackett's world, or Dum Spiro's world, tells Watt nothing, and yet all.

Not that I have told you all I know, for I have not, being now a good-natured man, and of good will what is more, and indulgent towards the dreams of middle age . . . which were our dreams, whatever may escape us now and then in the way of bitter and I blush to say even blasphemous words and expressions, and perhaps also because what we know partakes in no small measure of the nature of what has so happily been called the unutterable or ineffable, so that any attempt to utter or eff it is doomed to fail, doomed, doomed to fail. (p. 61)

According to Arsene, Watt has come to the exit from one life and the promised entrance into a new world where he sits 'waiting for the first dawn to break'. A parody of Eden fills the first part of the long speech, a parody where man has journeyed, in mock-Eliot 'Ash Wednesday' way,

'all the old windings, the stairs with never a landing that you screw yourself up, clutching the rail, counting the steps'

and has taken the last exit out of our world:

all the delights of urban and rural change of place, all the exitus and redditus, closed and ended. (p. 38)

In this special place he is in the right place at last, a place which fits him perfectly and which promises harmony, a journeyer no longer towards a destination he can never understand, but an arriver at the perfect place, when all outside will be he, the flowers, the flowers that he is among him, the the sky the sky that he is above him, the earth trodden the earth treading, and all sound his echo. When in a word he will be in his midst at last, after so many tedious years spent clinging to the perimeter. (p. 39)

All would be well, and we would have come home to Grasmere with Wordsworth and nature's mystics were this not in fact false. The victim, the next in the long alternating line of victims or slaves to Mr Knott, will feel that he is finally, fully and victoriously himself, defined at last; he sits down, says Arsene, 'proffered all pure and open to the long joys of being himself like a basin to the vomit'. Now he will have a function, a set of defining functions, to serve Mr Knott, Mr Knott's household and himself, and this, he knows, will be joy. Then, at one moment in time, something will happen, though nothing will have happened.

The sun on the wall, since I was looking at the sun on the wall at the time, underwent an instantaneous and I venture to say radical change of appearance. It was the same sun and the same wall, or so little older that the difference may safely be disregarded, but so changed that I felt I had been transported, without my having remarked it, to some quite different yard, and to some quite different season, in an unfamiliar country. . . . But in what did the change *consist*? What was changed, and how? What was changed, if my information is correct, was the sentiment that a change, other than a change of degree, had taken place. What was changed was existence off the ladder. Do not come down the ladder, Ifor, I haf taken it away. (p. 42)

Existence off the ladder was changed. What this may mean has led to some critical debate, but if, one may assume, Arsene had climbed up 'the stairs with never a landing that you screw yourself up' to a place where all ladders end, like Yeats's, in the rag-and-bone shop of the heart, into himself and had arrived at that romantic stasis so beloved of Keats where passion is unfulfillable, then existence is back where it was. He has not arrived anywhere and his rejoicing in his expanded spirit which united him with his outside had deceived him. 'The old thing where it always was, back again' and the romantic change of Daphne into a Laurel which at least was an escape from rape in the present to a permanency in a beautiful myth and an undying shrub is reversed, a 'reversed metamorphosis'. This is not Rocquentin's vision of Being, in the garden looking at the chestnut tree, in Sartre's *La Nausée*, an existential credo—but rather the world refusing the easy assimilation of itself into man in order that man can know himself or define himself in such a way as to leave no anguish, no unease. Arsene's questions are

left unanswered, though the prediction is made, obliquely, that something of the sort will happen to Watt. Something might happen to
Watt if Watt were encompassed by Arsene's words, by Arsene's voluble
and dexterous rhetoric which is cynical and bitter, disillusioned and
revelatory of the disappointed mystic who thought he had at last
reached the centre of existence. Arsene knows that his hopes are unfulfilled and that is all he can take with him

from this state or place on which my hopes so long were fixed. (p. 47)

He retains his clarity, his expertise with words, his cunning at coining
and his academic poise among 'intenerating considerations', his 'void
and bony concavity which my dear tutor used to say reminded him of
Crecy', his 'dianoetic laugh' and his 'Daltonic visualisations of the
morning paper's racing programme'. He dismisses himself from Mr
Knott's house and from Watt's presence in a parody of the Anglican
confession and a *nunc dimittis* blasphemously mocking the dying Lear:

Now for what I have said ill and for what I have said well and for what I have
not said, I ask you to forgive me. And for what I have done ill and for what
I have done well and for what I have left undone, I ask you also to forgive
me. And I ask you to think of me always—bugger these buttons—with forgiveness, as you desire to be thought of with forgiveness, though personally
of course it is all the same to me whether I am thought of with forgiveness,
or with rancour, or not at all. Good night. (p. 62)

What he has learnt from his time in Mr Knott's establishment cannot
be obvious, though his voice sounds the authentic Beckettian bitter
laugh. None the less, whatever assertions might have been made by
Arsene, endorsed by the author by his lack of comment, swallowed by
the reader, are allowed to stand only for a time. As there is a shifting
foundation for the novel, so everything shifts in Arsene's speech when
we read the authorial footnote to p. 79. There all is withdrawn by an
omniscient author whose omniscience is galling to the reader; Watt is
not like Arsene, but Arsene's assertions about refuge were, as Watt's
might have been, subject to 'fancies' or 'a similar eleventh hour vision,
of what might have been'.

'For it is scarcely credible that a man of Arsene's experience could have
supposed, in advance, of any given halt, that it was to be the last halt.' (p.
79, f.n.)

He who laughs last, in Beckett, laughs most seriously.
    How does Watt fit into this pattern that the novel lays down for him

to follow? Can Beckett provide such an articulate antecedent and not allow Watt to fit simply into the arithmetic series of retainers? Can there not be a sense that Watt must be one of the last of the series of the initial consonants if the names of the alternate retainers is adverted to:

Vincent,	Walter,	
Arsene	Erskine	Watt

We should be able to predict from the information we are given that Vincent and Walter were images of Watt ('very much your weight, breadth and width, that is to say big bony shabby seedy haggard knock-kneed men, with rotten teeth and big red noses') and say that Watt's successor will be like him too and have a name alphabetically lower than Watt's. And to say, too, that following him will come a vowel-opening name, beginning with I ('Ifor'?) and so on. Not true. Watt's successor is Micks (p. 215) and the symmetry which Arsene's information misled us to is truly false. There is a successor to Erskine who 'resembled Arsene and Erskine, in build. He gave his name as Arthur. Arthur' (p. 148). Again, a vowelled name, A as in Arsene. So, the prediction is not so clear. What is the control in all this? How random is this artificially contrived series, and why does Micks go back in the alphabet. What Micks will be like we have little idea, but Arthur certainly has the academic stamp on him, and his story of Ernest Louit and his dissertation The Mathematical Intuitions of the Visicelts fills twenty-eight pages and is left unfinished, putting him ahead of Arsene whose stamina is strong but not so strong as Arthur's. Yet Erskine is silent. So, there can be no rule about vowels and volubility, though there may be. All we can say is that Watt is another integer in a series which, though senseless, has enough about it to satisfy and leave un-appeased an appetite for law, order and symmetry. Just as the Unnam-able invents a fable for himself of a 'little job', a job of emptying one vessel and filling another:

'with my thimble I'd go and draw it from one container and then I'd go and pour it into another, or there would be four, or a hundred, half of them to be filled, the other half to be emptied, numbered, the even to be emptied, the uneven to be filled, no, it would be more complicated, less symmetrical, no matter, to be emptied, and filled, in a certain way, a certain order, in accord-ance with certain homologies, the word is not too strong, . . . (p. 401)

There are homologies, not identities, and Watt's world conducts itself within asymmetrical symmetries. They are fearful symmetries and

Watt is subjected to songs which promise symmetry but only show what Susan Field Seneff calls 'a study in unrelation'.[1] The song Watt hears in the ditch (pp. 32–4) shows time reducing, in its first verse, 'to decimal notation a leap year expressed in weeks ($52 \cdot 2857142857142\ldots$).[2] The second verse ($51 \cdot 1428571428571\ldots$) seems to be echoing the 'true ciphers' of π ($3 \cdot 142851, 142857, 142857\ldots$),[2] but also gives the leap year (366) minus a week (358) divided again into weeks, but omitting the first two decimal places ($51 \cdot [57]1428571428571\ldots$). We can predict the rest of the verses if we wish, though the end of the second verse would both allow and disallow this: '*till all the buns are done/and every-one is gone/home to oblivion*'. We can say that there will be 52 verses and a verselet. The verselet will be the odd one day of the leap year and this will be expressed as a value of 7, namely $\cdot 1428571428571$ into infinity, having arrived at the unending end. We can move from week to week in division because we arbitrarily stop the division sum and proceed to the next division by 7 but when there's no more dividing a larger sum than 7 we must go on into infinity by dividing 1 by 7. What mathematical aesthetic beauty promises in ideal relationships of number is aborted in a toneless and empty harmony. There is no whole beauty, only partial beauty, and its connection with reason and fact is obscure if not simply non-existent. Watt's choice between the two possible explanations of his finding the back door of Mr Knott's house open at his first entrance when he had first found it locked is settled on what are called 'aesthetic principles'.

Of these two explanations Watt thought he preferred the latter, as being the more beautiful. (p. 35)

That is, he opts for the possibility that someone opened the door rather than the possibility that he was simply mistaken in thinking the door locked in the first place. But 'the more beautiful' must mean the more difficult, as Watt offers more unanswerable possibilities to himself while contemplating the 'beautiful' alternative:

For if someone had opened the back door, from within, or without, would not he Watt have seen a light, or heard a sound? Or had the door been un-locked, from within, in the dark, by some person perfectly familiar with the premises, and wearing carpet slippers, or in his stockinged feet? Or, from without, by some person so skilful on his legs, that his footfalls made no

1. Susan Field Senneff, 'Song and Music in Samuel Beckett's *Watt*' in *Modern Fiction Studies*, XL, 2, Summer 1964, pp. 137–49.
2. Hugh Kenner, *Samuel Beckett*, 1961, pp. 104–5.

sound? Or had a sound been made, a light shown, and Watt not heard the one or seen the other? (ibid.)

But beauty in speculative possibilities has no connection with finding out in our normal sense. For 'the result of this was that Watt never knew how he got into Mr Knott's house'.

This aestheticism Kenner equated with pedantry:

Watt, who inhabits the house of Mr Knott in a kind of weak-eyed speculative daze, illustrates the principle that the pedant is the supreme aesthete (Lyly; Wilde), and so that every use of language sufficiently comprehensive and explicit tends, at the expense of brevity, to aesthetic status. (p. 98)

But 'aestheticism' is more than pedantry; it is a failing, and it inevitably leads to puzzle and a closed world of ideas, possibilities, words and situations dislocated. Man has fallen off the ladder of existence into the closed world of the mind. The mind contemplates its own activity and becomes less and less dependent on 'events' outside it; it withdraws into solipsism. But put this solipsistic, self-sufficient mind into its ideal place where speculative possibilities are not simple alternatives revolving round an open and locked door but tend towards the infinite, then *Watt* results. Put Watt into control, make him responsible for the solving of problems, and his own question-feeding mind will be at its finest and most absurd. Set him, a theological ruin, into what Jean-Jacques Mayoux finely calls 'the terrifying ruins of religious feeling'[1] and the results are frighteningly comic. Put him into the problems raised by Mr Knott's food and the disposal of the uneaten food into 'the dog's dish' when there is no dog, and ingenuity of construction shines brightly lunatic from the pages of *Watt*. No questions are raised by the complex nature of Mr Knott's food, only of how to dispose of the uneaten portion of the regular meals by a dog when no dog is kept by Mr Knott. There is no information as to how Watt becomes acquainted with the exact ingredients of the 'mess, or poss', nor how to proceed in its preparation.

For he knew, as though he had been told, that the receipt of this dish had never varied, since its establishment, long long before, and that the choice, the dosage and the quantities of the elements employed had been calculated, with the most minute exactness. . . .' (p. 85)

This is 'received doctrine' and by the observation of the ritual or rites is as rigid as the Old Testament laws:

1. 'Samuel Beckett and Universal Parody', translated by Barbara Bray, *Samuel Beckett: A Collection of Critical Essays*, Ed. Martin Esslin, *Twentieth Century Views*, 1965, p. 77.

This refusal, by Knott, I beg your pardon, by Watt, to assist at the eating, by the dog, of Mr Knott's remains, might be supposed to have the gravest consequences, both for Watt and for Mr Knott's establishment. (p. 113)

Yet nothing happened: 'No punishment fell on Watt, no thunderbolt, and Mr Knott's establishment swam on, through the unruffled nights and days, with all its customary serenity.' But perhaps 'nothing happened' because Watt's offence against the prescribed and immemorial rites was no real transgression; perhaps he was forced to transgress and

then he was at pains to transgress in such a way, and to surround his transgression with such precautions, such delicacies, that it was almost as though he had not transgressed at all. *And perhaps this was counted to him for grace* [my italics]. (p. 114)

But for Watt, as for all of Beckett's major figures, punishment would be a solace because at least it would imply relationships, fixities, order, and he would have a place and someone would be observing and taking account of his actions. As Jean-Jacques Mayoux well says:

In *The Unnamable* Beckett is explicit about the oppression we prefer to postulate in our own image rather than admit our absolute solitude and total and absurd responsibility. (op. cit., p. 78)

Man needs the fiction of punishment for a crime uncommitted in order that he bear up under the burdens of an emptiness and an isolation which are unbearable but must be borne. And the way that man has of bearing it, or at least that Watt is endowed with to bear it, is a conversion table. All events, in order that they can be accepted by Watt, must be made into words. Once they are in a system of ordered words, preferably in a mathematically precise formula, then they cease to be interesting, disturbing or contradictory. They are not put into words in order to explain themselves, to deliver a meaning or even a clue to 'reality'; they are only words. Watt's concern with the food and the dog is a passing concern and soon ceases to interest him.

Once Watt had grasped, in its complexity, the mechanism of this arrangement, how the food came to be left, and the dog to be available, and the two to be united, then it interested him no more, and he enjoyed a comparative peace of mind, in this connexion. (pp. 114–15)

So far, a problem of some complexity, a logistical problem, has been solved satisfactorily by the investigation, institution and refinement on an elaborate reciprocating system with variables to be allowed for.

And this parodies all complex machinery for apparently simple opera-
tions, and we appreciate it on this level. What we are not prepared for
in all of this is Watt–Knott. Watt knows that all he has done is to play
with the surface, but what more to the problem can there be? What
potential significance can lie behind the levite's ritualistic problems?
Watt knows that something remains untouched by his solution to
what he takes to be the problem set, some significances which he can
never put into words and therefore, in his sense, can not exist, yet exist
they do.

Not that for a moment Watt supposed that he had penetrated the forces at
play, in this particular instance, or even perceived the forms that they up-
heaved, or obtained the least useful information, concerning himself, or Mr
Knott, for he did not. But he had turned, little by little, a disturbance into
words, he had made a pillow of old words, for his head. Little by little, and
not without labour. (p. 115)

Watt, then, as Jacqueline Hoefer claims, is 'like the positivists' and
has 'an obsessive interest in language'.

Thought and language are identical for him. Thought is not a shadowy
activity of the mind which takes place prior to articulate expression. Whether
language be expressed internally or orally, thinking is the process of using
language. ('Watt', Samuel Beckett: *A Collection of Critical Essays*, Ed. Martin
Esslin, p. 62.)

Whatever confronts Watt is not meaningful, though names exist for
things, and he feels the 'need of semantic succour . . . at times so great
that he would set to trying names on things, and on himself, almost as
a woman hats', and he can sometimes find the words to say 'that is
what happened then', but the real meaning of anything must elude him,
leaving him only his dual inheritance as a man of the 'time-honoured
names' and his reason. And this reason is an instrument for sorting and
ordering the possible, but works strictly and mathematically. It makes
no leaps, makes no intuitive connections, no imaginative interpreta-
tions or symbolic relationships; Watt is someone satisfied with a
meaning 'the most meagre, the least plausible', someone

who had not seen a symbol, nor executed an interpretation, since the age of
fourteen, or fifteen, and who had lived, miserably it is true, among face values
all his adult life, face values at least for him. (p. 70)

The novel presents, through Watt, the meaning of meaning. Poor
Watt's mathematical mind which can see events most meaningfully

(for him) when they are safely tucked into a series, as he himself is part of a series of Knott's retainers, cannot easily cope with an incident which, if it is to be understood, must be so in terms of the unique, the individual and not the series. When, for example, he contemplates the picture in Erskine's room, one of the questions which disturbs him is the uniqueness of the painting, whether it was 'a fixed and stable member of the edifice' or whether it figured only as 'a manner of paradigm, here today and gone tomorrow, a term in a series, like the series of Mr Knott's dogs, or the series of Mr Knott's men, or like the centuries that fall, from the pod of eternity' (p. 129).

But because the picture belongs to Mr Knott's house it cannot be a fixity, for here nothing is fixed, and yet one has to reconcile the reasoning and the conclusion given in reverse order:

A moment's reflexion satisfied Watt that the picture had not long been in the house, and that it would not remain long in the house, and that it was one of a series. (p. 129)

Prolonged and irksome meditations forced Watt to the conclusion that the picture was part and parcel of Mr Knott's establishment. (p. 128)

What Watt has to achieve in his reasoning is the move from his 'moment's reflexion' to his 'conclusion' via his 'prolonged and irksome meditations'. And these involve reflexion on the whole nature of Mr Knott's establishment which would indeed be irksome for a mind like Watt's. How can he cope with the metaphysics of this world, a world which seems to point, as A. J. Leventhal cunningly claims, to the thought of the sophist Gorgias:

For the metaphysical background [to the Beckett canon] we must turn to a Sicilian rhetorician and sophist who flourished from 483–375 B.C.: Gorgias of Lentini. *The Encyclopedia Britannica* sums up his teaching thus:
1. There is nothing which has any real existence.
2. That even if anything did exist, it could not be known.
3. That supposing real existence to be knowable, the knowledge would be incommunicable.
In arguing the third of these propositions the philosopher says that language is inadequate to convey ideas and that it is impossible for any idea to be the same in different minds. ('The Beckett Hero', Samuel Beckett: *A Collection of Critical Essays*, Ed. Martin Esslin, p. 46.)

Mr Leventhal claims that the novel is comprehensible within the terms offered by the three propositions of Gorgias:

Mr Knott is the nothing of the first proposition. Should it happen to exist then he cannot be known and the final proposition makes it clear that his existence cannot be expressed in speech. Watt's language finally breaks down. He inverts the order of words, the order of letters and ends in incoherence. (p. 47)

Watt is a Beckettian cousin to Swift's Man, who is not a rational animal, but an animal capable of reasoning, *capax rationis*, or close to Rochester's Man:

> Huddled in dirt the reasoning engine lies
> Who was so proud, so witty and so wise.

We are here at some tether's end and Watt is the question man is reduced to asking, not the 'why' of scientific rationalism, nor the 'how' of technocracy, but the primary and basic question about 'reality'. We have to return to the beginning which is the only direction you can move in if you have come to the end, but retain fragments of a mathematical logic which demands order, series, and infinities, life as a 'matrix of surds'.

Watt engages his mind in the search for answers to problems which he feels to be presented to him, expends a great amount of cerebral energy on them, as, for example, the long series of hypotheses and the interrelated concepts of absurdity and necessity which are involved in the debate within himself as to the probable length of duration as servant on the ground floor and the first floor (pp. 130–4). In order for the problem to be solved we need to know how long in fact Watt spent on each of the two floors. From this we might construct an hypothesis as to the general law of duration for servants of Mr Knott, but this would need more information about other servants' duration. We could say that if Watt spent one year on the ground floor, then his predecessor must spend one year on the first floor (though he might have spent longer on the ground floor), and if Watt spent one year on the first floor then his successor must spend one year on the ground floor (though he might spend longer on the first floor). We would need to step outside the small series which contains Watt and move higher or lower up the larger series of Mr Knott's servants, 'a chain stretching from the long dead to the far unborn' (p. 132).

We could have saved Watt his energy, but that's all. He is condemned to 'the ancient labour'.

So at first, in mind as well as body, Watt laboured at the ancient labour.
And so Watt, having opened this tin with his blowlamp, found it empty.

As it turned out, Watt was never to know how long he spent in Mr Knott's house, how long on the ground-floor, how long on the first-floor, how long altogether. All he could say was that it seemed a long time. (p. 134)

The reason for something being as it is is either necessary or absurd, and absurd will mean contingent. The necessary will be arbitrary and the absurd will just be as it is because it is as it is. To look for laws among contingencies is absurd, to look for contingent reasons among the necessary equally so. Watt is caught in a Beckettian trap by being made a seeker after an absolute which, if it exists, cannot be expressed in words, and if it exists we cannot know it. Mr Leventhal is right, but very rightly wrong. He's wrong because Mr Knott and Watt do have a theological relationship.

Watt, even after leaving Mr Knott's house and having come closer to nothing, closer to sickness, poverty, and isolation, still has flickers of his old self, still falls into his 'old error' of asking 'Watt' things are 'in reality'. At the station wicket he sees a figure approaching which neither grows 'in height, in breadth or in distinctness' and the most that we know is that it is a Watt-figure, a doppelganger who seems dressed like Watt (see pp. 216–17), in

the uninterrupted surfaces of a single garment, while on the head there sat, asexual, the likeness of a depressed inverted chamberpot, yellow with age, to put it politely. (p. 225)

So, Watt sees himself approaching himself, and he is charged by the mood with wanting to know what is impossible to know, but at least he sees the error of his ancient ways, and this is a test for him. He can see himself from the outside and leave it at that; he can be emptied of self:

Who being in the form of God, thought it not robbery to be equal with God: But emptied himself, taking the form of a servant, being made in the likeness of man, and in habit found as a man, He humbled himself, becoming obedient unto death: even to the death of the cross. (St Paul to the Philippians, II. 6–8)

So, Watt partly becomes conclusively the parodic Christ figure that he had been foreshadowed earlier in the book. And the other part of Watt needs only to realise that he can only make mistakes by asking for metaphysical information about essences, rather than simply noting and forgetting existences:

For Watt's concern, deep as it appeared, was not after all with what the figure was, in reality, but with what the figure appeared to be, in reality. For since when were Watt's concerns with what things were, in reality? But he was for ever falling into this old error, this error of the old days when, lacerated with curiosity, in the midst of shadowy substance he stumbled. This was very mortifying, to Watt. (p. 226)

2

MORIBUNDS IN THEIR COURSES:

Molloy, Malone Dies, The Unnamable

What Beckett traces in the course of this trilogy of novels is the search for self, a hunt for identity by writers through writing. By choosing characters who all pursue a meaning for their existence and who can be seen in states of decay and asylum from the ordinary world, Beckett more and more closely approaches the problem of the writer who uses writing in order to avoid the eventually inevitable task of facing himself. But facing oneself, if one's existence is only that of a writer of stories, is facing that which will constantly escape definition when all the stories are taken away.

The trilogy is a gradual approach towards the problems of the nature of the self, the nature of language, the nature of creation. All provisional answers must be discarded, all provisional foundations dismantled.

Molloy

Beckett's trilogy *Molloy*, *Malone Dies* and *The Unnamable* proceeds thematically in two different directions: the search for self is pursued through the metaphor of the hunter and victim, and through the gradual narrowing down of the search for self by elimination of the world of men, of bodily functions, of the writer writing, to the voice speaking, vainly attempting the impossible articulation of 'I'.

Molloy, the first novel, can be viewed in many ways, but one might start by recognising the search for the self in the other. Molloy has searched for his mother's room and has returned to it, not to her who died as he returned, and he now has the task of telling himself, of telling his story, writing it out for another who comes on Sundays to take away his manuscript. His story is circular, takes him no further from his beginning, and leaves him simply remembering his journey which would have been interminable but for outside interference, call it help:

Well I suppose you have to try everything once, succour included, to get a complete picture of the resources of their planet. (p. 91)

But he remains where he is, sunk in a ditch, and memories and thoughts and questions turn in his head, but he has lost interest in all of it, most of it, and he dismisses himself from his work by the impersonal:

Molloy could stay, where he happened to be.

I have chosen to look at the ending of the first section of the work because it seems clear that this section refuses to come back to the beginning of the work and refuses to progress beyond that beginning. The way is open for the man, imprisoned in his cage of a room, immobile and waiting for the end to his existence, of the man who has to live in the present, has to pass the time *now*, has to progress beyond reminiscential story-telling. This, of course, will be *Malone Dies*.

But what is even more striking than the open end of the story of Molloy is the sense that the story of Moran should be read simultaneously with that of Molloy. Moran has to search and find Molloy for reasons unknown, but he ends up by becoming Molloy, becoming a man in a room writing of his search, writing his version of the myth, recognising that he has constructed a fiction, a necessary version of some truth which he has yet to uncover or discover. At the end of his 'report' which in the beginning was said to be demanded, presumably on the analogy of other 'reports' in the past (p. 137, 'Youdi must have had some way of verifying. Sometimes I was asked for a report . . .'), we learn that this time another 'voice' told Moran to write this 'report'.

I have spoken of a voice telling me things. I was getting to know it better now, to understand what it wanted. It did not use the words Moran had been taught when he was little and that he in turn had taught to his little one. So that at first I did not understand what it wanted. But in the end I understood this language. I understood it, I understand it, all wrong perhaps. That is not what matters. It told me to write the report. (p. 176)

Then we see that the whole of the 'report' is false, all invented, all fiction.

Then I went back into the house and wrote, It is midnight. The rain is beating on the windows. It was not midnight. It was not raining. (ibid.)

What we are left with is the recognition that the two halves of *Molloy* are strangely related, curiously linked, mirror-images one of the other, and that Molloy/Moran is a unit, that as Molloy is Moran will be. The two characters are related as obverse and direct image. As Molloy is shy of people, inefficient in dealing with people and affairs, disorientated and internally occupied, so Moran is a man of affairs, a parody of the secret agent, knowledgeable about people, concerned with questions, formulae, tabulations, and is sadistic and domineering. Molloy searches for the mother for whom he has a complex tenderness and revulsion.

I called her Mag because for me, without my knowing why, the letter g abolished the syllable Ma, and as it were spat on it, better than any other letter would have done. And at the same time I satisfied a deep and doubtless unacknowledged need, the need to have a Ma, that is a mother, and to proclaim it audibly. (p. 17)

Moran's concern is with his son, the reflection of the father with the same name, Jacques Moran ('This cannot lead to confusion'), and the only reflection on his mother is curiously linked with Molloy's mother, and with a selection of the earlier fictional heroes of Beckett's world in a catechetical list of questions:

9. Would I go to heaven?
10. Would we all meet again in heaven one day, I, my mother, my son, his mother, Youdi, Gaber, Molloy, his mother, Yerk, Murphy, Watt, Camier and the rest? (p. 168)

Mirror-images, but sharing details of experience and of physique. It is part of Moran's startling decomposition that his legs start to stiffen and become useless, necessitating the use of crutches, like Molloy, and he, like Molloy, uses a bicycle for part of his progress. It is also part of the similarity between these two protagonists that they both have an acute sense of hearing, have similar uncertainties about the colours blue and green, and, oddly, appear to have a similar testicular condition. Moran, on ascending his bicycle with the aid of his son who is pedalling, is anxious about this balancing act so badly enacted, so pitifully clownish:

The wheels began to turn. I followed, half dragged, half hopping, I trembled for my testicles which swing a little low. (pp. 157–8)

And, in the earlier, more metaphorical and lovingly detailed account of the internally orientated Molloy who explains why he was unable to help dig the grave for Lousse's dog by referring to his useless leg we are told

. . . I was virtually one-legged, and I would have been happier, livelier, amputated at the groin. And if they had removed a few testicles into the bargain I wouldn't have objected. For from such testicles as mine, dangling at mid-thigh at the end of a meagre cord, there was nothing more to be squeezed, not a drop. So that *non che la speme il desiderio*, and I longed to see them gone, from the old stand where they bore false witness, for and against, in the lifelong charge against me. For if they accused me of having made a balls of it, of me, of them, they thanked me for it too, from the depths of their rotten bag, the right lower than the left, or inversely, I forget, decaying circus clowns. And, worse still, they got in my way when I tried to walk, when I tried to sit down, as if my sick leg was not enough, and when I rode my bicycle they bounced up and down. (pp. 35–6)

Both Molloy and Moran have a few moments of silent contact with a shepherd, his dog and his sheep. For Molloy it is in the morning and he asks a question of the shepherd which is ignored and then the whole procession moves off leaving Molloy watching them. What is important about this incident is that the shepherd and dog had been watching over Molloy 'and the shepherd watching me sleep and under whose eyes I opened my eyes' (p. 28), that this vague solicitude for Molloy by a shepherd who expects nothing and who speaks no word and shows no open friendship that may have many explanations from a pseudo-Biblical to the need to be witnessed (*esse est percipi*) passes into Molloy. He is troubled by thoughts of suffering, the suffering of the dumb animal, as just before he had heard angry cries and dull blows alongside the canal and then

My eyes caught a donkey's eyes, they fell to his little feet, their brave fastidious tread. (p. 27)

With the sheep his solicitude is extensive and concerned with their possible fate, which, by deliberate mistake on his part as to the method of killing sheep, is extended to all animals. The circle widens to take in the whole countryside and the breeding, killing and suffering involved in living.

That then is how that second day began, unless it was the third or the fourth, and it was a bad beginning, because it left me with persisting doubts, as to the destination of those sheep, among which there were lambs, and often wondering if they had safely reached some commonage or fallen, their skulls shattered, their thin legs crumpling, first to their knees, then over on their fleecy sides, under the pole-axe, though that is not the way they slaughter sheep, but with a knife, so that they bleed to death. But there is much to be said too for these little doubts. Good God, what a land of breeders, you see quadrupeds everywhere. (p. 29)

This is the 'mollose' Molloy, tender-hearted but instinctively seeking identification and common cause with the victim of life's blows, who would, impotent, 'mollify' or lessen the harshness of life's condition for sufferers.

On the other side, Moran's encounter with a shepherd is at the other end of the day, at evening, and he leaves his son to approach the shepherd to ask the way to Ballyba. The event is proclaimed by Moran in terms of his own longing to be taken into service, to be cared for, to be released from himself. Quite obviously we are being shown the impossible temptation for Moran of escape into a simple pastoral with the unafraid 'flock of black shorn sheep' and its capable but taciturn and peaceful shepherd.

How I would love to dwell on him. His dog loved him, his sheep did not fear him. Soon he would rise, feeling the falling dew. The fold was far, far, he would see from afar the light in his cot. Now I was in the midst of the sheep, they made a circle round me, their eyes converged on me. Perhaps I was the butcher come to make his choice. . . . I longed to say, Take me with you, I will serve you faithfully, just for a place to lie and a little food. (p. 159)

The event, too, reverberates in Moran's imagination, and his thoughts are turned not, as were Molloy's, to the suffering sheep destined for slaughter, but to the shepherd, complete and content in his pastoral idyll, needing no one and safe in his own little world.

And so no doubt they would plod on, until they came to the stable or the fold. And there the shepherd stands aside to let them pass and he counts them as they go by, though he knows not one is missing. Then he turns towards his cottage, the kitchen door is open, the lamp is burning, he goes in and sits down at the table, without taking off his hat. But the dog stops at the threshold, not knowing whether he may go in or whether he must stay out, all night. (p. 160)

Moran ends with the faithful dog, the condition he would apply for if it were vacant because his concern is with himself, the ego dominant; Molloy sees the procession go off and is not concerned with himself as safe or saver, he is emptying himself of himself.

The shepherd is not the only common denominator in the complex equation of $M/n \rightleftharpoons M/n$: they share in their assault of someone each meets in the forest. Molloy's assault is framed in a turbulence of reminiscence about his time in the forest and he seems to remember a charcoal burner, old like himself, as incoherent and incomprehensible as himself, a simulacrum of himself. He inclines, without much evidence, to the hypothesis (one of four) that 'he wanted to keep me near him ... for when I made to go, he held me back by the sleeve' (p. 84). After felling him with 'a good dint on the skull' with his crutch, he carefully and with some pain uses his crutches as pivots to work up his body into a pendulum swing and launch himself backwards on to the body 'since he had not ceased to breathe'. With his 'mania for symmetry' this 'homo mensura' takes up his position on the other side of the body for a second assault. The cruelty of the assault resides in the fabrication of the mechanics of the motion by the imagination which could well have been satisfied by the initial statement

'I contented myself with giving him a few warm kicks in the ribs, with my heels.'

But, granted the given condition of such legs with such heels, the complex mechanical manœuvres necessary to effect such punishment take over the forefront of the writer's imagination. With baroque enthusiasm for his telling he elaborates and makes internally credible by convincing detail the invented incident:

But I must have aimed a little low and one of my heels sank in something soft. However. For if I had missed the ribs, with that heel, I had no doubt landed in the kidney, oh not hard enough to burst it, no, I fancy not. (p. 84)

But in this complex writer's compendium of a narrative, no simple handle is held out for the critical reader. We are not allowed simply to say Molloy kills his own image on his journey of self-annihilation, nor simply to say that the fiction generates itself once the co-ordinates of a moribund *homo mensura* of no fixed abode are given, nor that we are here concerned with a case of schizophrenia. We recognise multiple parody as we might recognise multiple injuries or multiple sclerosis:

People imagine that, because you are old, poor, crippled, terrified, that you can't stand up for yourself, and generally speaking that is so. But given favourable conditions, a feeble and awkward assailant, in your own class what, and a lonely place, and you have a good chance of showing what stuff you are made of. And it is doubtless in order to revive interest in this possibility, too often forgotten, that I have delayed over an incident of no interest in itself, like all that has a moral. (pp. 84–5)

Here the incident is presented as instructive, as useful, as advancing a thought needful to be remembered: the writer as instructor in the line of Bunyan or Swift. All resolves itself into fictions, more or less parodic, but all proclaimedly lies.

Moran's encounter is quite different and suits his harder, more tightly vicious nature and reveals Moran to us very clearly indeed. This time Moran is the man with the fire and he is approached from behind by a man who, presumably, is bent on what Molloy feared, a homosexual encounter ('I could see he was precisely the kind of pest I had thought he was, without being sure, because of the dark', pp. 150–1). Several noticeable features in the incident need recording: the man is a simulacrum of Moran ('. . . the face which I regret to say vaguely resembled my own, less the refinement of course, same little abortive moustache, same little ferrety eyes, same paraphimosis of the nose, and a thin red mouth that looked as if it was raw from trying to shit its tongue', p. 151); he is searching for an old man with a stick; he is dressed as for the city and is obviously careful and fastidious about his apparel—all like the original Moran; Moran kills him by a blow on the head. All these features point to Moran's killing of his old image, but they all depend on the mental blackout that Moran has about how he killed. Moran sees a hand coming towards him opening and closing and

I do not know what happened then. But a little later, perhaps a long time later, I found him stretched on the ground, his head in a pulp. I am sorry I cannot indicate more clearly how this result was obtained, it would have been something worth reading. But it is not at this late stage of my relation that I intend to give way to literature. (p. 152)

Molloy has obviously 'given way to literature' while Moran is treating himself as a classical schizophrenic. One critic sees the explanation of much of Beckett's work as lying in his own interest in schizophrenia (G. C. Barnard, *Samuel Beckett: A New Approach. A Study of the Novels and Plays*, 1970), and of this passage in particular the critic says:

We can interpret this as a pure hallucination, the whole murder and subsequent description of how he disposed of the body and hunted for his scattered keys, dragging himself forward catatonically clutching the grass and rolling over and over, being enacted in phantasy. Or we may believe then an actual man was really attacked by the maniac who projected on to him his now features. In either case the important point is the initial identification of the man with the Moran personality which the emerging Molloy personality was trying to supplant. At the moment of the attack Moran suffered a blackout, for at that moment Molloy had gained control. This maniac fit, whose ferocity is emphasized by the fact that Moran found a torn off ear on the ground, marks the point where Molloy really gains the upper hand for a while, though he keeps it only temporarily. (op. cit., p. 36)

While we might not go all the way with Mr Barnard, we can certainly agree about the features he draws our attention to, the blackout, the catatonic condition, the identification of the Moran personality, but things are not quite so simple. Moran sees the image of himself as obscene and disgusting, yet, ironically, 'less the refinement of course'. This, if anything, is the image of a coarsening Moran who is changing and knows himself to be changing the whole time.

Question.   How did I feel?
Answer.   Much as usual.
Question.   And yet I had changed and was still changing?
Answer.   Yes.
Question.   And in spite of this I felt much as usual?
Answer.   Yes.

(p. 154)

Moran is changing, but his change is in the direction of Molloy, not into Molloy simply. He never arrives there. He is being himself, on the way to annihilation of Moran, perhaps to move into the next stage, Molloy. But his coming to himself after the murder is a coming back not simply into the 'Moran personality' but into being more like his 'old self' where he can bend his leg normally. Then, quite quickly, his leg is stiffening up again. 'It no longer required to be supple.' He is coming back into his new self which is again on its way to become Molloy. And, from what we know of Molloy, he is not the fierce savage that Mr Barnard would induce us into believing, but the person who has 'given way to literature'. Moran's nature asserts itself, the rage for order, the man with duties and responsibilities, who checks his pockets to see if anything is missing, who, at great personal expense of energy, recovers his scattered keys and broken key-ring, and repairs the chain and ring once again to accommodate his keys, the symbols of his property-oriented nature.

Moran is subject to irrational outbursts of rage and this is a climactic one. Molloy is shy of people but can be relied on to come through on his own terms most of the difficulties put in his way by his obtuseness, patience and basic unconcern for human beings and their world. Moran is a man of the world who tries to manage by an acquired *savoir vivre*, is a born manager and controller who is involved in a chain of command, of people knowing their places, knowing their station. But his being a man of the world is only the way of narrating what he calls 'the methods of my full maturity' (p. 133) and he has to recount the journey through 'the Molloy country' while he bears Molloy with him. The full complexity of Moran's relationship with Molloy cannot be accounted for in terms simply of a split personality, our psychological classic, the schizophrenic. Several pages of dense writing by Moran try to tell something of the relationship. In a kind of Murphy inspection of the mind, Moran dismembers reality and 'best pierce(s) the outer turmoil's veil'. Then he becomes like God, looking down on the universe and passing judgment on it all, and sees himself as the agent who can deliver man from some kind of bondage, 'as lonely and as bound' as the rest of the world in time's flux. The job of the hunter, the seeker that Moran is, is to give a meaning to the life of the victim who has been waiting for just this moment when he is singled out, having thought himself a being apart:

His life has been nothing but a waiting for this, to see himself preferred, to fancy himself damned, blessed, to fancy himself everyman, above all others. (p. 111)

Man, essentially alone and bound in time, awaits the impossible moment when something enters his life to give it an eternal significance (damned, blessed, everyman). But as we have Molloy's story already before Moran's, so Molloy is never found by Moran. Instead, Moran becomes Molloy in his turn and the function of giving meaning and eternal significance returns to man himself, and therefore becomes an impotent and impossible task. Because man can never find himself to save himself, man constantly invents others to fill the void of the controller, the one who enters, the intersection of the timeless with time. But Moran, at this time, only finds meaning in himself:

I drown in the spray of phenomena. It is at the mercy of these sensations, which happily I know to be illusory, that I live and work. It is thanks to them I find myself a meaning. (ibid.)

By withdrawing from phenomena and the course of the world into his mind Moran can contemplate Molloy. This region of contemplation is called 'the atmosphere, how shall I say, of finality without end, why not . . .', and we are not sure what 'finality without end' might mean, but it certainly says something about the impossibility of ending and, at the same time, the purpose (final cause) of the action which is to end the existence of the victim. Molloy is seen, in this sense, as being the man, lonely and bound, awaiting an impossible deliverance, as we have already seen in Molloy's own ending.

Fortunately for me at this painful juncture, which I had vaguely foreseen, but not in all its bitterness, I heard a voice telling me not to fret, that help was coming. Literally. (p. 91)

But, more than this, Molloy was 'no stranger' to Moran, and 'Mother Molloy, or Mellose, was not completely foreign to me either, it seemed'. But *how* Moran knows he does not know—'Perhaps I had invented him, I mean found him ready-made in my head'. And 'who could have spoken to me of Molloy if not myself and to whom if not to myself could I have spoken of him?' Not unexpectedly all this gives Moran great uneasiness, but, however, he knows about Molloy. He knows the whole schema of Molloy's existence.

He had very little room. His time too was limited. He hastened incessantly on, as if in despair, towards extremely close objectives. Now, a prisoner, he hurled himself at I know not what narrow confines, and now, hunted, he sought refuge near the centre. (p. 113)

This elliptic expression of Molloy's existence applies equally to the journey to his mother's room which is Molloy's narrative, and equally to the existential condition that Molloy is, man nearing the end, and coming closer and closer to finding himself after hunting himself, though escaping himself by seeking 'refuge near the centre'.

Such an understanding of what it means to be a Molloy can never be explained away by a rigid application of the conceptions of abnormal psychology, and must be accepted as part of the continuing explication by means of stories, fables, myths of what it means to confront oneself, to attempt to find 'I' behind all the words, behind the bric-à-brac of existence to meet the essence.

But, in the end, there are, for Moran's delectation, five possible Molloys: 'He that inhabited me, my caricature of same, Gaber's and the men of flesh and blood somewhere awaiting me. To these I would add Youdi's . . .' (p. 115). And the relationship between all of these versions of Molloy is problematical, not the least of which is the relation between 'the Molloy I stalked within me thus and the true Molloy' (p. 115). What Moran makes so unclear we must not try to schematise simply, and, though the Molloy within him may bear certain marks or characteristics in common with the 'true' Molloy, we must not simply equate them. What Moran's Molloy means to Moran is 'just the opposite of myself, in fact' (p. 114). He is huge in bulk like a bear, swaying beast-like to and fro, uttering incomprehensible words:

Then I was nothing but uproar, bulk, rage, suffocation, effort unceasing, frenzied and vain. (p. 114)

This figure which haunts Molloy, unsettles him and disturbs his natural equanimity is not even 'the true denizen of my dark places', so that while the reader recognises that this apparition is *not* Molloy, he is also turned to face the allegation that Moran knows he is *not* his true Molloy, his true hidden Molloy. Moran had said earlier about the relationship of false terms in a premise when discussing the notional Molloy and the real Moran:

For where Molloy could not be, nor Moran either for that matter, there Moran could bend over Molloy. And though this examination prove unprofitable and of no utility for the execution of my orders, I should nevertheless have established a kind of connection, and one not necessarily false. For the falsity of the terms does not necessarily imply that of the relation, so far as I know. And not only this, but I should have invested my man, from the outset, with the air of a fabulous being, which something told me could not fail to help me later on. (p. 112)

And, should one try to work out some sensible scheme for understanding all this complexity of relatedness, we are pushed off our plank, head in hand, by Moran's throwing all of the terrible business away from himself onto the incomprehensible Youdi, the omnipotent tyrant whose orders must be obeyed and who runs the organisation of which Gerber and Moran are two elements, messenger and private investigator.

And let us not meddle with the question as to how far these five Molloys were constant and how far subject to variation. For there was this about Youdi, that he changed his mind with great facility. (p. 116)

So, Moran and Molloy are linked, but their coupling is not easily understood, neither is it demonstrated in terms of one man finding another, only one kind of person, Jacques Moran, gradually losing everything, accelerating into the condition of the moribund, and returning to his empty and derelict home a changed man. But Moran, who had been attached to *his* things, his bees, his hens, his religion, now finds in place of his bees 'a dry light ball', finds also that his hens are all dead, and goes on to reject Father Ambrose.

One day I received a visit from Father Ambrose. Is it possible! he said when he saw me. I think he really liked me, in his own way. I told him not to count on me any more. He began to talk. He was right. Who is not right? I left him. (p. 176)

His nature is altered and now, having jettisoned his impedimenta, he is presumably free to go to encounter Molloy, to encounter himself facing his own end alone.

I am clearing out. Perhaps I shall meet Molloy. My knee is no better. It is no worse either. I have crutches now. I shall go faster, all will go faster. They will be happy days. I shall learn. All there was to sell I have sold. But I had heavy debts. I have been a man long enough, I shall not put up with it any more, I shall not try any more. (p. 176)

Now he is ready to become Molloy, but his own Molloy. The outer, the man, the Jacques Moran, man of property and bourgeois proprieties will be no more.

But, in the end, the whole of Moran's narration had been compulsory, a task, a penance, variously said to be demanded by Gaber, by Youdi and the third person, and by Moran himself, and, more than all this, had been invented to fulfil certain requirements. It is all lies, and, in the end, despite Moran's claim, literature.

Malone Dies

Following *Molloy*, *Malone Dies*. Moran had been set in motion to try to find Molloy, find Molloy within himself, to bring himself to such an abject condition where succadanea of possessions, religion, comforts, son, are jettisoned so that he can come closer to the real state of himself, conveniently called Molloy, unaccommodated man, and yet Moran remained self-confessedly a fabrication, a 'contrivance' (p. 114). The couple Molloy–Moran had been an unsuccessful metaphor for the mind, the twin conditions of mind, empty and full, new and familiar, the journey within explored as a journey without:

I did as when I could not sleep. I wandered in my mind, slowly, noting every detail of the labyrinth, its paths as familiar as those of my garden and yet ever new, as empty as the heart could wish or alive with strange encounters.

And I heard the distant cymbals, There is still time, still time. But there was not, for I ceased, all vanished and I tried once more to turn my thoughts to the Molloy affair. Unfathomable mind, now beacon now sea. (p. 106)

The metaphor had been unsuccessful because the mind had searched for itself in metaphors which were credited as being more than metaphors, as being the search itself, and the reasons for the search for itself have been pushed onto an authority which lies outside the mind. Molloy's progress has been enlivened by what he calls his imperatives and he has been forced by 'convention' to say things which are merely the equivalents of conditions within the mind which are unsayable:

And when I say I said, etc., all I mean is that I knew confusedly things were so, without knowing exactly what it was all about. And every time I say, I said this, or, I said that, or speak of a voice saying, far away inside me, Molloy, and then a fine phrase more or less clear and simple, or find myself compelled to attribute to others intelligible words, or hear my own voice uttering to others more or less articulate sounds, I am merely complying with the convention that demands you either lie or hold your peace. For what really happened was quite different. (pp. 87–8)

With Moran, the 'fact' is that he may never achieve even the condition of the Molloy personification in the recognition of the nature of his work as fictional. He may tell the necessary lies, necessary for his condition, but his narrative will be much more self-consistent, much less fractured with distrust of the fiction, and he has a long way to go before he comes to the single room and the declared condition of the writer writing. Molloy still retains the authority from outside himself urging him to write, and preventing him (for the moment) from doing what he would like most.

What I'd like now is to speak of the things that are left, say my good-byes, finish dying. (p. 7)

And so, it is the delayed work of 'finishing dying' that, suspended for the novel *Molloy*, becomes the *modus operandi* of the second work, *Malone Dies*: 'And that was the end of sweet Molly Malone'.

Ma(n) alone is responsible for what he writes and there is no more evasion in responding to the question 'Who made me?': Youdi(d). Gone is the external apparatus of either the mother's womb-room wished return, or of the authority, absurd and compelling, of Youdi through Gaber to Moran. Now the mind can be held responsible for what it turns out in the way of fiction. There is a very revealing comment at the very beginning of *Malone Dies* where the second paragraph looks back over the range of Beckett's early fiction and obliquely gives us some distinction well worth the having. Earlier fiction had been playing 'with what I saw', and this fiction will be 'play(ing) with myself'.

J'ai conçu Molloy et la suite le jour où j'ai pris conscience de ma bêtise. Alors, je me suis mis à écrire les choses que je sens.[1]

When the sense of fiction involves the writer as part of the fiction we have critical problems. One finds it hard really to come to a clear understanding of, say, *Tristram Shandy*, without using critical conveniences like 'persona' to account for the incorporation of Sterne, the novelist, in his novel under the guises of Parson Yorick and Tristram himself and at the same time keeping Tristram and Yorick as 'characters' who are created out of elements of Sterne himself. Critics argue about the identity of Tristram and Laurence Sterne, but it seems clear that we have here a fictional work which delights archly in confusing the reader and playing with existing conceptions of fiction. Similarly, but without the waggishness of Sterne, and without the rather simple mocking of the reader in the Sternean manner of *Murphy* ('Try it sometime, gentle skimmer', p. 60), *Malone Dies* (and *The Unnamable*) conflates Beckett the writer and the speaking, temporary, eponymous hero of the novel. That is, the speaker is not simply one in a line of writers (Sam in *Watt*, Molloy, Moran) but is the writer of all those who have gone before.

Then it will be all over with the Murphys, Merciers, Molloys, Morans and Malones, unless it goes on beyond the grave. (p. 237)

Moran had been the residue of the writer of stories, including one unpublished by Beckett (*Mercier et Camier*)[2] and one not told by Beckett (Yerk).

Oh the stories I could tell you if I were easy. What a rabble in my head, what a gallery of moribunds. Murphy, Watt, Yerk, Mercier and all the others. I would never have believed that—yes I believe it willingly. Stories, stories. I have not been able to tell them. I shall not be able to tell this one. (p. 138)

This full revelation is held back for a good part of the work, but the second paragraph obviously can refer to the playful creation and then

1. Interview with Gabriel d'Aubarède, *Les Nouvelles Littéraires*, 2 February 1961, quoted by Ludovic Janvier in *Pour Samuel Beckett*, pp. 43–4.
2. Eventually published in Paris, Editions de Minuit, 1970.

suspension *in vitrio* of Mr Hackett in *Watt*, the hunchback of un-
pleasing appearance and behaviour:

This time I know where I am going, it is no longer the ancient night, the
recent night. Now it is a game, I am going to play. I never knew how to play,
till now. I longed to, but I knew it was impossible. And yet I often tried. I
turned on all the lights, I took a good look all round, I began to play with
what I saw. People and things ask nothing better than to play, certain animals
too. All went well at first, they all came to me, pleased that someone should
want to play with them. If I said, Now I need a hunchback, immediately one
came running, proud as punch of his fine hunch that was going to perform.
It did not occur to him that I might have to ask him to undress. But it was
not long before I found myself alone, in the dark. That is why I gave up
trying to play and took to myself for ever shapelessness and speechlessness,
incurious wondering, darkness, long stumbling with outstretched arms,
hiding. Such is the earnestness from which, for nearly a century now, I have
never been able to depart. From now on it will be different. I shall never do
anything any more from now on but play. No, I must not begin with an
exaggeration. But I shall play a great part of the time, from now on, the
greater part, if I can. But perhaps I shall not succeed any better than hitherto.
Perhaps as hitherto I shall find myself abandoned in the dark, without anything to play with. Then I shall play with myself. To have been able to conceive such a plan is encouraging. (pp. 180–1)

One could identify crucial elements of *Watt* from this speech, as one
could talk of the 'earnestness' of Watt, Molloy and Moran. This time
the writer/creator will be acknowledgedly 'playing'. His 'play' will be
self-satisfying, have apparently no other purpose than the writer's
playing himself out, playing out his life so that he can finish dying.
Now there will be no more involvement with what is said, no emotional
heat, no interest above the level of the academic in what is said, as there
will be no more anguish and no more delight. The aim seems to be a
stoic's turning all the gauges of the human being's apparatus as low as
possible.

Yes I shall be natural at last, I shall suffer more, then less, without drawing
any conclusions, I shall pay less heed to myself, I shall be neither hot nor
cold any more, I shall be tepid. I shall die tepid, without enthusiasm. (p. 180)

This writer is self-sufficient and all that he has will be reviewed in
sufficient time for all of him to be left behind at the point of death. His
creativity and his own history can be exorcised simultaneously; he can
spit on himself and his own status and situation by proxy, can reject the
ideals and the facets of humanity and leave them behind. His relationship with others is acidly scorning, and there is no Nunc Dimittis calm

c

about Malone. What he can do is review his present state, tell a few stories and make an inventory of his possessions.

Because he is a character as well as a creator he has several problems. The first one, of course, is that he can not be sure when his moment of death will come, and this means that any scheme he has of filling in the time it takes to die will be absurd. It will fill the time (anything would) but it can always be true that anything that is started may never be finished, and equally true that 'four stories' may be too many, too few, or just enough.

However, because the author, Beckett, has constructed the writer, a contrivance called Malone, the limits of the fictional world are not as fluid and indeterminate as is said.

And, again, the problem that this duality raises is no worse than the problem which the central metaphor of *Malone Dies* presents. If a man is recording his dying in a notebook with a pencil, then one of three things can happen:

    (a) he will run out of paper;
    (b) he will run out of pencil;
    (c) he will have sufficient paper and pencil.

But, even should he be able to continue writing his story and finish its telling with his very last pencil stroke on his very last gasp, he and we would have to subscribe to the 'fiction' that he, Malone, is a character who is defined only by his writing the words we read in a book (and not this book but a child's exercise book). But we can see, even from within the book *Malone Dies*, that we are listening to a voice which is saying as well as inventing. The 'saying' is written (for us) but this is not the inventing which Malone 'writes' down. So, for example, we might say that the *writing* only starts on p. 183. We are introduced to the voice ruminating, the self considering itself and the strategy to be consumed in order to pull off the job of writing the dying. The conclusion of the meditation, a soliloquy we are privileged to hear, ends with the voice determining to stop 'thinking' and to get on.

'If I start trying to think again, I shall make a mess of my decease.' And, with a firm purpose of amendment, the voice resolves:

To return to the five. Present state, three stories, inventory, there. An occasional interlude is to be feared. A full programme. I shall not deviate from it any further than I must. So much for that. I feel I am making a great mistake. No matter.
          Present state. This room seems to be mine.   (pp. 182–3)

So, the retelling of *Molloy* starts. This time we have the room, the writing and the voice, but without the attempt to keep Molloy as a consistent character, a fictional unit. But resemblances insist on intruding from work to work. Molloy had made some sense out of his chaotic experiences by inventing (or telling) the story of his stay with Sophy Lousse, flowing together bits and pieces into an amalgam ('For all things run together, in the body's long madness, I feel it', p. 56). He creates a situation where he is imprisoned and has all needs catered for, is conscious of the eyes spying on him, and is allowed the run of the garden and is equally conscious that the whole of his story of his stay with Lousse is false.

> If I go on long enough calling that my life I'll end up by believing it. It's the principle of advertising. (p. 53)

He has therefore used the whole complex story of Lousse, modelled upon the benign insane, incarcerated (for his own good) in a hospice for the insane, as a vehicle for his incomprehension of this business of living in the mind.

> And these different windows that open in my head, when I grope among those days, really existed perhaps and perhaps do still, in spite of my being no longer there, I mean there looking at them, opening them and shutting them, or crouched in a corner of the room marvelling at the things they framed. (pp. 51–2)

The metaphoric situation of the hospice for the mad is widespread and endemic in Beckett's fiction, but altering in status from the early *Murphy* through *Watt* to the trilogy. Here it is an incompletely satisfying metaphor for the condition of the mind, isolated from others, bodily needs catered for, even love thrown in for good measure, but craving the knowledge of itself, and finding only a *cacoethes scribendi*, a rage for writing with no subject for the writing, with nothing to say. Isolation, self-sufficiency and the pencil and paper.

Malone draws on the madhouse as did Molloy. Malone may be in an institution (as might Molloy) though he is careful to establish the normality of the house he inhabits, though signs are there to the contrary. Not many rooms in many ordinary houses have the kind of spartan equipment and regimen as Malone's. The madhouse is reserved for his fictional creation, MacMann, who is allowed to lead the final story into the final dissolution of Malone. MacMann will carry the final freight of bitterness and anguish in Malone's world, and Moll will be the culmination of female protectress, wardress, loved ones, the visitors who penetrate the outer ramparts of the inner world of man. She survives from Watt's Mrs Gorman, and, in some special way, from Molloy's story of his love-affair with Ruth ('I think, but I can't say for certain. Perhaps the name was Edith', p. 56). It is perhaps a story stimulated in Malone's creative imagination by his declared situation where an old woman attends to his modest needs.

The woman came right into the room, bustled about, enquired about my needs, my wants. I succeeded in the end in getting them into her head, my needs and my wants. . . . I believe her to be even older than I. But rather less well preserved, in spite of her mobility. Perhaps she goes with the room, in a manner of speaking. But it is conceivable that she does what she does out of sheer charity, or moved with regard to me by a less general feeling of compassion or affection. Nothing is impossible, I cannot keep on denying it much longer. (pp. 185–6)

One might say that to conceive of Malone in a room entails some organisation, however primitive, to keep him going, to keep him dying, and that she went with the room 'in a manner of speaking'. To say that Malone *is* in an institution is to deny the status of Malone who is not a character in a realistic or even psychological novel (or even a metaphysical novel in the Kafka mode). But, to say that Malone is capable of using the items of experience which he might have had, had he an existence, is about as far as we might go. We might then say that Malone, in this sense, would be capable of re-inventing himself as A. N. Other Man, son of man, MacMann, who is in an institution and whose existence is brightened, if that is the word, by love, if that is the word, of Moll, his keeper.

The story Malone tells is grotesque and savage, a bitter condemnation of romantic erotica and designed for Malone's own ends.

She seems called upon to play a certain part in the remarkable events which, I hope, will enable me to make an end. (p. 258)

What part she plays is hard really to define. She is part, certainly, of the vision of mankind as grotesque and clown, and, in part, a last despairing look at human need and tenderness. For with the obscene and the ugly goes the tenderness; if one then the other. With the 'sombre gratification' of the sex, 'given their age and scant experience of carnal love', go the love letters, of which we are given one example, from Moll to MacMann, and the versicles, of which we are given two

examples, from MacMann to Moll. But every positive has its concomi-
tant negative in Beckett's later fiction. So, we are not allowed to dismiss
Moll and MacMann as a rather pathetic, comic and grotesque last love
affair (which it is) without the whole picture being much more complex.
Malone, like Vladimir in *Waiting for Godot*, has been interested in the
saving of one of the thieves by the dying Christ, and, just before he
takes up MacMann's story for this last canter, he said:

I must have fallen asleep after a brief bout of discouragement, such as I have
not experienced for a long time. For why be discouraged, one of the thieves
was saved, that is a generous percentage. (p. 256)

So, in the Moll-creation she becomes parodic of the Crucifixion scene,
complete with thieves, though the element in the scene likely to change
is the representation of Christ and not the thieves. She has the scene on
her person:

She wore by way of ear-rings two long ivory crucifixes which swayed wildly
at the least movement of her head. (p. 258)

And, later, she says

with a smile (she smiled at the least thing), Besides they are the thieves,
Christ is in my mouth. Then parting her jaws and pulling down her blobber-
lip she discovered, breaking with its solitary fang the monotony of the gums,
a long yellow canine bared to the roots and carved, with the drill probably,
to represent the celebrated sacrifice. With the forefinger of her free hand she
fingered it. It's loose, she said, one of these fine mornings I'll wake up and
find I've swallowed it, perhaps I should have it out. She let go her lip, which
sprang back into place with a smack. (p. 265)

The parody blasphemously mocks Moll and MacMann, the overtones
of such an extended image reverberate, and we cannot see Moll in any
mutedly advantageous light again. Just after this Malone feels that she
has to die. In one way one might say that the way mankind has of
needing salvation, of abusing any salvation or saviour it gets or invents,
makes man a doubly pitiful creature. Malone sees MacMann as a stage
further back along the road of emptying oneself. He has desires
aroused in him, remembers the Crucifixion story, is even able to penetrate 'into the enchanted world of reading' (p. 261), and, in sum, is far
worse off than if he had been Ma(n) alone. Therefore, Malone can look
forward to the one who will succeed him who will have even less
burdens than he has.

Weary with my weariness, white last moon, sole regret, not even. To be
dead, before her, on her, with her, and turn, dead on dead, about poor mankind, and never have to die anymore, from among the living. Not even, not
even that. My moon was here below, far below, the little I was able to desire.
And one day, soon, soon, one earthlit night, beneath the earth, a dying being
will say, like me, in the earthlight. Not even, not even that, and die, without
having been able to find a regret. (p. 265)

Malone is among the living and his sole regret is that he cannot be one
with the dead moon; another will come who will be dying alone and
not 'from among the living', who will not even be able to regret.
Disdainfully, then, he can 'will' Moll when she loses her tooth. Love
dies, Christ comes out, and

One morning early a man whom he had never seen came and told him that
Moll was dead. There's one out of the way at least. My name is Lemuel, he
said, though my parents were probably Aryan, and it is my charge you are
from now on. Here is your porridge. Eat it while it is boiling. (p. 267)

From now on, with 'a last effort', cruelty takes over with the entrance
of the sadistic Lemuel and Malone's artistic problem is how to keep
the story going so that he can finish it off completely. Nearing the end,
Malone revises his programme and wants the artistic success to be
complete, however difficult it might be.

Here is the programme anyhow, the end of the programme. . . . Here it is.
Visit, various remarks, MacMann continued, agony recalled, MacMann continued, then mixture of MacMann and agony as long as possible. It does not
depend on me, my lead is not inexhaustible, nor my exercise-book, nor
MacMann, nor myself in spite of appearances. That all may be wiped out at
the same instant is all I ask, for the moment. (p. 270)

Malone then recounts a visit from someone suspiciously like an undertaker: 'I took him at first for the undertaker's man' (though it is hard
to take him for anything else). Then, he follows his programme and
moves through his 'various remarks' to MacMann, though 'agony' is
more nearly true than 'remarks'.

   We are not allowed to see simply the man dying who creates stories
to pass the time; we are thrown into a confusing set of images, all
powerful, but difficult to relate one to another. MacMann is seen as a
pygmy looking out to the 'distant raging sea' and 'the others' watch
him or the sea expectantly. This image of the sea and threatened destruction is powerful and carries sufficient force to suggest isolation,
being helplessly witnessed and destruction near at hand: all ways of

projecting the speaker's approaching death onto a new version of MacMann (p. 275). Something is altering in Malone's mind; an innumerable babble, like a multitude whispering, is something new for Malone, and he cannot understand it. But the end is approaching; the pages are counted and they are deemed enough to finish his life: 'This exercise book is my life, this big child's exercise book, it has taken me a long time to resign myself to that' (p. 276).

After rest, MacMann's story is resumed with the threat of destruction neatly dropped but the MacMann of the outdoors is created. To get over the isolation, terrible in the previous paragraph, MacMann is credited with odd behaviour necessitating the keepers hunting the grounds for him. Malone seems unable really to make up his mind about Lemuel's relationship with MacMann, having sometimes moments of speechless tenderness huddled together with him in MacMann's special lair in a bush, and, again, senseless cruelty towards him. When Malone invents MacMann coming back to his cell 'with a branch torn from a dead bramble' he first allows Lemuel to take it from MacMann and strike him with it 'over and over again, no, that won't work', then

Lemuel called a keeper by the name of Pat, a thorough brute though puny in appearance, and said to him, Pat will you look at that. (p. 277)

The *raison d'être* of the new story is plain enough, MacMann pitifully at the mercy of the keepers and his need for beauty and tenderness rudely stamped on, and this accelerating into the operation of the mind finding legal solutions to an invented puzzle about why MacMann is punished, and then into a passage about the birds who inhabited the garden. But, says Malone,

All is pretext, Sapo and the birds, Moll, the peasants, those who in the towns seek one another out and fly from one another, my doubts which do not interest me, my situation, my possessions, pretext for not coming to the point. . . . Yes, there is no good pretending, it is hard to leave everything. (p. 278)

Malone must get on with his story of MacMann, start again, hurl himself into the telling by parodying Paradise, the Miltonic mountain with the plateau atop, the Coleridgean walled garden (even down to the stream that rises underground). He hates himself for his involvement in the story, but is none the less involved:

A stream at long intervals bestrid—but to hell with all this fucking scenery. Where could it have risen anyway, tell me that. Underground perhaps. In a word a little Paradise for those who like their nature sloven. (p. 279)

MacMann is now seen as vainly looking for an escape from the Paradise where all his needs are catered for and all his desires annulled, his faculties of memory and reflection 'stunned' into 'the black joy of the solitary way'. Malone is trying, but his creature MacMann can only be jettisoned when his life is over. Malone is the writer, the fabulist, and however much he desires to leave the whole howling fiasco of life behind through his surrogate, he cannot do it. What he has to do is to fill the forefront of his story with others, with other than MacMann, has to get on with inventing a way out for MacMann as he approaches his own death. The irony is that he can invent a cruel and murderous end, but not for MacMann, only for others. Against charity and sweetness he can take revenge, and he can have the generous and elderly Lady Pedal break her hip and lie groaning; he can have the keeper Lemuel butcher two sailors with an axe, but he cannot kill off MacMann.

The final words of the novel show Malone fighting for breath, fighting for his story and being unable to kill off his hero-victim. Adrift on the sea, in the night, in a huddle six bodies, their heads buried in their cloaks, remain, and Lemuel/Malone can kill no one any more.

The rhythm of the dying voices trailing off, the typographical conventions of a dramatic presentation of the state of the teller, all work towards an understanding of this ending as spoken. The writing is crucial, right enough, but it is the writing of the novelist Samuel Beckett, and not of the author, Malone. Where the short story 'The End' had allowed the speaker the fiction of the boat at sea being removed, and the final dissolution, we have here an unfinishable story, a story that can have no neat ending, however mythic, because the author's own writing ends not with death but with the loss of the last lights, the 'absurd lights', and the loss of the story. The author *qua* author is dead because there is no more story to tell, nor will there be any more of any story to tell, not simply this story of Saposcat–MacMann.

Malone Dies is the last of the fictions which try to reconcile the function of the story as calmative and as purgative, the story as invention out of the need to tell stories because they help to empty the writer of himself, of his relationship with people and things, in a word all that anchors him to the life of a man. Malone's stories, he predicted, would 'not be the same kind of stories as hitherto, that's all'.

They will be neither beautiful nor ugly; they will be calm, there will be no ugliness or beauty or fever in them any more, they will be almost lifeless, like the teller. (p. 180)

Needless to say, the intention spoken so well is frustrated; Malone becomes involved in his stories willy-nilly. They are himself writing out himself, and, as such, he can't let go easily. They all peter out, are inconclusive, become the mind's ineffectual doodling, a writer's play. Malone can no more leave creating fictions alone than he can stop being Malone, and the whole procedure whereby he and his creations, he and his child's exercise book, will be exactly coterminous, is frustrated. A necessary failure.

The Unnamable

All the novels in the trilogy make an attempt to begin and end. *Molloy* begins by offering the reader, not Molloy's biography, but only the beginning which Molloy said that he began 'like an old ballocks' but which 'they are keeping apparently' and over which the writer said he took a great deal of trouble. He says that he has forgotten half the words and forgotten how to spell, yet his 'story' is meticulously spelt and has a great weight of vocabulary. We are told, too, that the writer is still writing ('Is what I do now any better?') and, while we are brought to a terminus in Molloy's tale, being rescued unaccountably as he finally emerges from the forest, we are not brought back to the beginning of the narrative. The circle is not closed and the gap between being found and his career as a writer is profound. The Molloy we do not know is Molloy the writer and we only have an early example of his fiction, his 'beginning'.

Malone is a writer, too, whose *cacoethes scribendi* is unaccountable and mysterious and he is beginning to end. His whole function is writing and his nature is writer who avoids his own end by creating fictions through which he can escape, ineffectually.

The Unnamable opens with the necessity of starting again with the beginning, with the situation being presented of the writer writing. But this time we have questions in place of affirmative statements, questions which indicate the necessity of saying something in a situation where there is no certainty, not even a fictitious certainty. The voice has to speak, has to proceed, has to go on from a basis so insecure, so impossible, where there is no belief possible in a situation of time and place, no belief in a direction or purpose for the fictional procedure, no belief in the personal pronoun 'I', that to go on is sheer lunacy. We have a total dislocation of fictional telling, total abandonment of the necessary certainties; floundering in fragments becomes the fictional method of the opening of the work.

The voice tries to get a purchase on a story so that something can get under way. We find several different kinds of beginning before we come to *the* 'beginning'. We have, first, the attempt to answer the question 'how did it all start', by:

Can it be that one day, off it goes on, that one day I simply stayed in, in where, instead of going out, in the old way, out to spend day and night as far away as possible, it wasn't far. Perhaps that is how it began. (p. 293)

But, even without the deliberate undermining of the fiction by the doubts thrown in by the voice itself ('in where'), and by the recognition of the habit of telling stories ('off it goes on'), this is an abortive start. It won't work. This kind of approach is abandoned after a few lines of denial and doubts and the little discussion is cut off by 'These few general remarks to begin with'.

The questions then turn back on the possibility of proceeding and the limited methodological usefulness of moving on, 'by affirmations and negations invalidated as uttered, or sooner or later'. More questions, more denials, more undermining of the safety of the posture assumed ('I should mention before going on any further, any further on, that I say aporia without knowing what it means').

The next possible beginning proper is that where one thinks, as reader, that the self-conscious and self-analytic voice speaks with impossible confidence of the manner and method of the impossible task of this writer. He speaks of that which he cannot speak of; he is abandoned; the voice trails away.

The fact would seem to be, if in my situation one may speak of facts, not only that I shall have to speak of things of which I cannot speak, but also, which is even more interesting, but also that I, which is if possible even more interesting, that I shall have to, I forget, no matter. (p. 294)

So, unlike the philosopher who could indulge in methodic doubt and emerge with the aid of angelic intelligence and *Cogito ergo sum* into the luminous world of Cartesian certainty, this mind is flawed and cracked, a sad instrument when judged by Descartes' standard: *Cogito: quaere sum? Sum? Cogito?*

After this abandoned beginning and the conclusion of the opening paragraph, we come, as in *Molloy*, to *the* beginning. This time the writer sees the course of his narrative as being one, like Moran's, of decreasing, of abandonment. Where Malone had failed by depending upon his fictions, this writer will succeed in failing better by progressive loss of his fictions. He declares himself in the same tradition as Malone, playing with creatures, but, where Malone had talked of 'people and things', who 'ask nothing better than to play' (p. 150), this writer can speak of his 'puppets'. And whatever turns up in the way of things, he says, will be fortuitous. Where Malone's model had been the child in the magic world of the playroom, calling his people and things to him deliberately and authoritatively, the model is now one where the writer is the victim of circumstances over which he has no control.

If a thing turns up, for some reason or another, take it into consideration. (p. 294)

The whole world of people and things which can be 'scattered to the winds' is suffered, chosen as the way to begin, though he is quite plain that 'The best would be not to begin. But I have to begin. That is to say I have to go on' (ibid.).

We have this urge to write, the nothing to write of and the nothing to write, which is the final point to which the fictional world of the trilogy drives. Some illumination may be gained by recognising that Beckett was firmly convinced in 1949 that the art he thought most highly of was the art of failure. In a dialogue with Georges Duthuit published in *Transition*,[1] on the painter Bram van Velde, Beckett's recorded conversation went:

B. —The situation is that of him who is helpless, cannot act, in the event cannot paint, since he is obliged to paint. The act is of him who, helpless, unable to act, acts, in the event paints, since he is obliged to paint.
D. —Why is he obliged to paint?
B. —I don't know.
D. —Why is he helpless to paint?
B. —Because there is nothing to paint and nothing to paint with.
D. —And the result, you say, is art of a new order?

(pp. 119-20)

1. *Transition*, '49, no. 5; reprinted in 1965 by Calder and Boyars in *Proust and Three Dialogues with Georges Duthuit.*

Further, Beckett, in the same dialogue, draws a distinction between making the predicament of such an art expressive of the impossibility to express and 'the ultimate penury'.

But let us, for once, be foolish enough not to turn tail. All have turned wisely tail, before the ultimate penury, back to the mere misery where destitute virtuous mothers may steal bread for their starving brats. There is more than a difference of degree between being short, short of the world, short of self, and being without these esteemed commodities. The one is a predicament, the other not. (p. 122)

Therefore, we can discern a programme for *The Unnamable*: a course of impossible fiction which will not simply be expressive of the difficulty of saying with nothing to say and nothing to say it with, but will be a work of art 'of a new order', a work of artistry based on 'the ultimate penury'. The writer, unnamable, will have literally nothing, no place, no time, no 'I', no one hiding at the centre. He will construct provisional and rickety versions of place, time, situation, I, others, a centre, a past, a voice, but there will be behind all this the doubtful ability of words to spawn and make themselves, to give meaning just by being words. *The Unnamable*'s *raison d'être* will, of course, be writing, but the writing itself will have nothing to offer the writer. And the double nature of the voice will be essentially self-frustrating, for this voice will be both that of the former creator of the creatures in past Beckett fiction, most immediately Malone of the previous novel, and a creature in succession to them all, the next in line,

To tell the truth I believe they are all here, at least from Murphy on, I believe *we* [my italics] are all here, but so far I have only seen Malone. (p.295)

But alongside this impossibility lies another: this voice, this impossible cipher, is that which underlies all the other ciphers in Beckettian fiction. He claims that all the others were merely his vice-existers.

I am neither, I needn't say, Murphy, nor Watt, nor Mercier,—no, I can't even bring myself to name them, nor any of the others whose very names I forget, who told me I was they, who I must have tried to be, under duress, or through fear, or to avoid acknowledging me, not the slightest connection. (p. 328)

But the invention of Murphy and the rest was something ineffectual and crude; Murphy's voice wasn't his own because you could see the ventriloquist, and Murphy and the rest were 'bran-dips' who made him waste his time, 'suffer for nothing, speak of them when, in order to

stop speaking, I should have spoken of me and of me alone' (p. 305).
These other creatures were barriers to reaching the Unnamable who
says that he was always

on the premises, within easy reach, tottering under my own skin and bones,
real ones, rotting with solitude and neglect, till I doubted my own existence,
and even still, today, I have no faith in it, none, so that I have to say, when
I speak, Who speaks, and seek, and so on and similarly for all the other
things that happen to me and for which someone must be found, for things
that happen must have someone to happen to, someone must stop them.
(p. 394)

But not so fast. This voice is that of the creator of former fictions, and
the voice that was being untrue to itself by escaping vicariously into
fictions. But, stripped of fictions, emptied of creatures, what is left?
Obviously, one can say that the writer, Beckett, is facing himself and
his situation as artist denying himself his art as fabulist and testing
himself. But this would be too easy, and false into the bargain. The
voice is not Samuel Beckett's own voice, but a fictitious and autonomous voice, the master of the fictions, the unattainable meaning of the
previous fictional appearances. This is the real substance; they were
individuations whose matter became the substance of their tales;
essence and existences.

Well, if they ever succeed in getting me to give a voice to Worm, in a
moment of euphory, perhaps I'll succeed in making it mine, in a moment
of confusion. There we have the stake. But they won't. Did they ever get
Mahood to speak? It seems to me not. I think Murphy spoke now and then,
the others too perhaps, I don't remember but it was clumsily done, you could
see the ventriloquist. And now I feel it's about to begin. They must consider
me sufficiently stupefied, with all their balls about being and existing. Yes,
now that I've forgotten who Worm is, where he is, what he's like, I'll begin
to be he. (p. 351)

The problem might be stated thus: the urge to write and make stories
is mysterious, and the writer makes stories to satisfy himself, therefore
his stories are, in some special sense, the writer himself. If the writer is
honest, the argument runs, he is also seeking something, chasing an
elusive meaning, and the more he tries, the further he goes, the nearer
he may come to this elusive meaning which is himself. The tempta-
tions besetting the writer are twofold: he may simply enjoy playing
with his creations (playing including revenge against life or the
mother who, bearing him, condemned him to life) or he may slip into

the pretence that he is his creation and play out the life of his creation-victim vicariously (the Malone condition). What this involves the Unnamable in is the impossible situation, the unbearable situation where, as creative fabulist, he must jettison all the modes of fictional meaning one by one to reach himself. For his test is to end, to finish the whole business of making, to find himself, at last, behind all the words, behind all the creatures, behind the supporting myths.

So, the way of presenting solitude and impotence first occurs as a complex little myth, compounded of versions of Hell and torment. Fixed immovably in space, eyes open with the motionless figure of Malone in profile (or perhaps it is Molloy, wearing Malone's hat) passing regularly in front of him like a moon going round its earth, the Unnamable creates himself. Slowly accretions follow, more and more the situation resembles the mind landlocked in a failed body, and having only the eyes to inform it of the present, but living its inner life with whatever rags of information remain about life in the world of men to work on, but work on it must.

What puzzles me is the thought of being indebted for this information to persons with whom I can never have been in contact. Can it be innate knowledge? Like that of good and evil. This seems improbable to me. Innate knowledge of my mother, for example, is that conceivable? Not for me. She was one of their favourite subjects, of conversation. They also gave me the low-down on God. They told me I depended on him, in the last analysis. They had it on the reliable authority of his agents at Bally I forget what, this being the place, according to them, where the inestimable gift of life had been rammed down my gullet. (p. 300)

But the situation here offered would make the voice that of a mythic enactment of the mind, a philosophical parable. This won't do for the Unnamable. Having tried that particular version, he complicates the issue by obliquely making it obscurely clear that he is now engaged on a later version of *Malone Dies*. 'But the days of sticks are over,' he says, 'here I can count on my body alone, my body incapable of the smallest movement and whose very eyes can no longer close as they once could, according to Basil and his crew . . .'. And, in this cessation of motion, the Malone dead, the immediate question, delayed for a while, is that of how the writer can then write. The answer could be invented, the difficulty solved in any of the prestidigitations of the other fictional writers in the trilogy, which they are so given to, but there is no answer this time:

How, in such conditions, can I write, to consider only the manual aspect of that bitter folly? I don't know. I could know. But I shall not know. Not this time. It is I who write, who cannot raise my hand from my knee. It is I who think, just enough to write, whose head is far. (p. 303)

This time we have only the puzzles, and no solutions which are only palliatives anyway. The thing needful is to get 'myself' born into the fiction, to be able at last to go silent with the fear of at last going silent, and 'my' appealing model of solitary impotent struggling must be discarded. So, 'my' temptation to see the artist's work as 'obliging humanity' must be dismissed. That way lies an art of the artist 'obsessed with his expressive vocation' and where 'everything is doomed to become occasion' for his art ('Bram van Velde', op. cit., p. 124), and in this case any temptation to see the artist as Prometheus must be discarded:

For between me and that miscreant who mocked the gods, invented fire, denatured clay and domesticated the horse, in a word obliged humanity, I trust there is nothing in common. (p. 305)

All models for the artist in this spiritual suffering and epistemological poverty are to be discarded, as must 'all these Murphys, Molloys and Malones', formerly enlisted as 'sufferers of my pains'. So, by a process of gradual questioning of the possible being that I am, the area of likelihood narrows from a man, to a round ball carried on shoulders, 'a great smooth ball I carry on my shoulders, featureless, but for the eyes, of which only the sockets remain' (p. 307). Then to a ball, or perhaps a cylinder or an egg, and then only a voice. And then the voice which flows on, flows without control, pitiless, remorseless, which is not 'mine':

It issues from me, it fills me, it clamours against the walls, it is not mine, I can't stop it, I can't prevent it, from tearing me, racking me, assailing me. (p. 309)

Time and again the voice seeks some kind of bitter consolation in the thought that he is being witnessed, being watched, being tested by 'others', that there is a 'master' who might have controlled him, or even 'a whole college of tyrants, differing in their views of what should be done with me, in conclave since time began or a little later, listening to me from time to time, then breaking up for a meal or a game of cards' (p. 312). This was the consolation, in part, of Malone whose Youdi and his messenger, Gaber, allowed Malone not to be free, to be excusable, to be responsible to others, not to himself.

Meanwhile, in order 'not to peter out', he may well have 'to invent another fairytale, yet another, with heads, trunks, arms, legs and all that follows, let loose in the changeless round of imperfect shadow and dubious light' (pp. 309–10). So, to keep going he needs to create a fiction, snatched from almost nothing, plucked out of the air as it were. Basil is turned from a manipulator into a toy to be manipulated in his turn. He had first appeared as one of the 'persons' who had presented their report, so-called, on men and the world. This had roused the hatred of the Unnamable because 'he changed me a little more each time into what he wanted me to be' (p. 300), and he was therefore a kind of manipulator of the essence who individuated it into an individual existence. Revenge would be to manipulate the manipulators, but it is a case of the manipulator manipulated:

Decidedly Basil is becoming important, I'll call him Mahood instead, I prefer that, I'm queer. It was he told me stories about me, lived in my stead, issued forth from me, came back to me, entered back into me, heaped stories on my head. I don't know how it was done. I always liked not knowing, but Mahood said it wasn't right. He didn't know either, but it worried him. It was his voice which has often, always mingled with mine, and sometimes drowned it completely. (p. 311)

And Mahood has made his entrance. But, unlike Malone's stories, deliberately chosen and functioning with a special purpose for the writer, fulfilling special needs, Mahood is coterminous with the speaker, and one is almost thrown back upon the schizophrenic to account for this. But this would be too easy. What is apparent, none the less, is that the Mahood both is, and is not, the Unnamable. He is a story-teller who heaps his stories on the Unnamable's head and is more like Malone or Molloy than anything. But, this time, the Unnamable can take revenge upon all the storytelling by making Mahood in his own image and likeness. Instead of the round ball he can re-enact the 'armless, legless, chickenless egg' of the folk song 'Oh Johnny I hardly knew you', but he can tell the whole set of little stories which go under Mahood as being Mahood's stories. Moreover, the temptation for the Unnamable actually to become Mahood and for that reason to become closer to the human is what 'they' throw in his way. 'They' want him to suffer as a sacrificial human being, to become at last

'One of us at last! Green with anguish! A real little terrestrial! Choking in the chlorophyll! Hugging the slaughterhouse walls! (p. 318)

The need to define the creation of *alteri Christi*, of other victims, is pushed onto others, but this is a subterfuge, an uneasy attempt to define the non-freedom of the artist. Mahood's story is an old one ('Mahood himself nearly codded me more than once') and so, being already known, can be slipped into at any point that the writer chooses and, equally, slipped out of again. The progress of Mahood's story will then be irregular and problematical, having some consecutive spurts and bearing the inquisitive and questioning mind of the narrator's effort to understand both the *modus operandi* of the tale, the fable, and his own status. Mahood is caught at the end of an impossibly long and comic journey (the *ne plus ultra* of all the journeys in the trilogy), one-legged and anxious to return to the bosom of his family which perishes of food poisoning as he circles about their dwelling in his helicoidal motion:

At the particular moment I am referring to, I mean when I took myself for Mahood, I must have been coming to the end of a world tour, perhaps not more than two or three centuries to go. My state of decay lends colour to this view, perhaps I had left my leg behind in the Pacific, yes, no perhaps about it, I had, somewhere off the coast of Java and its jungles red with rafflesia stinking of carrion, no, that's the Indian Ocean, what a gazeteer I am, no matter somewhere round there. (p. 319)

But, such details, invented here and tested by the mind as it invents, accepting and discarding possibilities, are seen as part of Mahood's own cunning at usurping the tale and introducing more and more circumstantially credible details. The leg, for example, left in an exotic jungle, later was possibly missing before 'I' left home ('My missing leg didn't seem to affect them, perhaps it was already missing when I left', p. 321), but to bolster the credibility of the tale other voices are introduced, other witnesses of the narrator's actions. When the family has been elegantly disposed of in two sentences, the narrator realises the folly of using up his story so quickly and has to deny that ending, at least for a while, and hit the ball up again:

According to Mahood I never reached them, that is to say they all died first, the whole ten or eleven of them, carried off by sausage-poisoning, in great agony. Incommoded first by their shrieks, then by the stench of decomposition, I turned sadly away. But not so fast, otherwise we'll never arrive. (pp. 320–1)

So, starting up again, the narrator falls into a trap:

That's one of Mahood's favourite tricks, to produce ostensibly independent testimony in support of my historical existence. (p. 321)

But Mahood's presence in the little inner drama of who is telling whom is neatly complicated by the Unnamable's momentary uncorrected mistake of quoting Malone as Mahood.

The answer to all that is this, I quote Malone, that I was . . . (p. 322)

And the story, such as it is, can be reinforced at any point with new developments, with the impossible next stage of decomposition casually introduced.

I must really lend myself to this story a little longer, there may possibly be a grain of truth in it. Mahood must have remarked that I remained sceptical, for he casually let fall that I was lacking not only a leg, but an arm also. (p. 323)

The joke is that the writer inventing the whole also invents Mahood whose story is only a story, but the Mahood in the impossible story tries to make the writer believe this incredible farrago by twisting the story in more and more impossible directions. The writer, having accepted a piece of information (mal- or mis-information) uses it, manipulates it and proceeds further into the deepening comic pit.

With regard to the homologous crutch, I seemed to have retained sufficient armpit to hold and manoeuvre it, with the help of my unique foot to kick the end of it forward as occasion required. (pp. 323–4)

And, like a woman trying on hats, the writer tries various different endings for this little story—one where he turns back from the agony and corpse smell, one where he savagely stamps 'under foot the unrecognisable remains of my family, here a face, there a stomach as the case might be'. The ending is either the one where he ends 'the last days of my long voyage in mother's entrails', or that where he devours 'what remained of the fatal corned beef'. He forgets the difficulty of his one leg for stamping (as Molloy had done but extricated himself by a commodious fiction) and that the original version was sausage-poisoning. Other versions, other stories, the one impossible story, and all nonsense.

But enough of this nonsense. I was never anywhere but here, no one ever got me out of here. (p. 326)

But, in order somehow to get rid of 'them and their contraptions' constantly pressing in on the Unnamable to bring him into the condition of moderately despairing humanity, having finite sufferings mercifully cut off, he feels he must tell 'another of Mahood's stories', and, this time, no more movements, no more family, no more journeys, no more than a trunk, 'Stuck like a sheaf of flowers in a deep jar, its neck flush with my mouth, on the side of a quiet street near the shambles, I am at rest at last' (p. 329).

The metaphor of the slaughter-house takes physical shape, and the original metaphor for the isolation and immobile fixity of the Unnamable takes on this impossible bottled condition, observed by eyes, the 'pupilless eyes of stone' of a 'statue of the apostle of horse's meat' and 'those of my creator, omnipresent, do not imagine I flatter myself I am privileged'. The neatness of the ambiguity of 'creator', the Unnamable himself as the teller of himself, Samuel Beckett as the only begetter, and God, the omnipresent, should not stop us, but should claim our attention momentarily.

At rest in his jar, Mahood lives out his little fictitious life with 'clear and simple notions' as a parody of Cartesian mind with its 'clear and simple ideas', a pathetic mute with a savage turn of phrase directed against himself, others and the world, but whose story is fragile in its telling, liable to be lost or forgotten by the teller. A remnant of an educated mind hangs on as long as it can in the telling of the tale.

De nobis ipsis silemus, decidedly that should have been my motto. Yes, they gave me some lessons in pigsty Latin too, it looks well, sprinkled through the perjury. (p. 332)

But the longer it goes on the more credible it becomes, hateful truth:

This story is no good, I'm beginning almost to believe it. (ibid.)

And the Unnamable is thrown into perplexity by the recognition that the gap between the two versions of Mahood, the wanderer and the jar, may be hints left to the Unnamable to fill in, 'hoping to induce in me the illusion that I had got through the interval all on my own', and adorning him with existence. Perhaps, the thoughts go, it was necessary for him to be 'given a taste of two or three generations', that all the previous fictional existences he had endured, back to 'that kind of youth in which they had to give me up for dead' (Belacqua and Murphy), have been pretexts 'to get me out of here'. 'They' are the guilty ones, but the superintendent of them all is the most guilty, the tormentor who will not give me quittance until they have abandoned me as inutilisable and restored me to myself. (p. 333)

This, presumably, is the God-creator-tormentor, Samuel Beckett, but it is not known, and Mahood takes up again, casually without introduction, one voice sliding into the other.

Soon at my present state of decrease, I may spare myself this effort. And spare myself the trouble of closing my eyes, so as not to see the day, for they are blinded by the jar a few inches away. (pp. 333–4)

Endlessly churning words pour out of the mouth which denies that it is a mouth; stories are lost, taken up, retold and the Unnamable fights constantly against being made human, however truncated, however nearly inanimate. Mahood, so apparently inhuman that he may perhaps be unnoticed by anyone, not even a dog, though in full public view in his jar advertising the bill of fare in Madeleine's chop-house, may have only a tentative identity. He may only exist as a figment of Madeleine's imagination:

No, there is no getting away from it, this woman is losing faith in me. And she is trying to put off the moment when she must finally confess her error by coming every few minutes to see if I am still more or less imaginable in situ. (p. 346)

And Mahood's stories are finally abandoned (for the moment) and the next stage is the creation of Worm, the creature whom the Unnamable thought to be at least a step towards himself, being larval or embryonic, incapable of sensing, without the possibility of thought. But even this is a subtle temptation:

To think I saw in him, if not me, a step towards me! To get me to be he, the anti-Mahood, and then to say, But what am I doing but living, in a kind of way, the only possible way, that's the combination. Or by the absurd prove to me that I am, the absurd of not being able. Unfortunately it is no help my being forewarned, I never remain so for long. (p. 349)

The creation of the conditions of Worm's existence in words unfortunately for the teller becomes the creation of more than a 'num dum blin' creature. It is as though the creation of a little less than nothing involves in it the creation of more than this little. Worm must be seen as the analogue of the teller, Worm is the teller, and 'others' are trying to entice Worm into their hands so that he can be saved from his own condition. The teller is placed in a quandary: either he carried on with Worm's story which can be no story, given Worm's condition of existence, or he faces his own condition, really confronts the emptiness that he is. The one way out of the quandary which is not taken up is that which is only later perceived in *Imagination Dead Imagine*, where nothing is capable of becoming, where the Imagination can no longer make nothing become something, where the two mirror images, geometrically sealed within a white dome, never come to fictional life. Here, it is a forlorn hope:

Quick, a place. With no way in, no way out, a safe place. Not like Eden. And Worm inside. Feeling nothing, knowing nothing, capable of nothing, wanting nothing. Until the instant he hears the sound that will never stop. (p. 351)

Behind the torment of the words and the impossible voice with the unanswerable questions is its problem of identity, the question of the relationship of the teller to his created personae:

Please God nothing goes wrong. Mahood I couldn't die. Worm will I ever get born? It's the same problem. But perhaps not the same personage after all. The scytheman will tell, it's all one to him. (p. 355)

To tell Worm is to become Worm, but to become Worm is to attempt to hide by being the teller told, to allow the fiction of 'others' assaulting the freedom of Worm and enticing him into existence so that,

finally, to wind up with, song and dance of thanksgiving by victim, to celebrate his nativity. (ibid.)

And Worm's story follows as a parable on human existence, being trained for life by successive stimuli, all intended to show how much freedom Worm has under his instructors. After torment

he'll be given lessons in keeping quiet. But for the moment let him toss and turn at least, roll on the ground, damn it all, since there's no other remedy, anything at all, to relieve the monotony, damn it all, look at the burnt alive, they don't have to be told, when not lashed to the stake, to rush about in every direction, without method, crackling, in search of a little cool, there are even those whose sang-froid is such that they throw themselves out of the window. No one asks him to go to those lengths. (pp. 370–1)

No, he has to learn (what the Unnamable has to) 'the alleviations of flight from self, that's all, he won't go far, he needn't go far' (p. 371). The condition of humanity, Worm, is bad enough, but the nothingness of the Unnamable is the worst imaginable. All he is is words, capable of spinning others:

give us time, give us time and we'll be a multitude, a thousand, ten thousand, there's no lack of room, *adeste*, *adeste*, all ye living bastards, you'll be all right, you'll see, you'd never be born again, what am I saying, you'd never have been born, and bring your brats, our hell will be heaven to them, after what you've done to them. (p. 382)

And whatever words pour out, even at 'six and eight the thousand flowers of rhetoric', and whichever way the 'wordy-gurdy' (p. 403) turns, all that is really there is a voice spilling words. Instead of a calm reconciliation in the face of the inoperable work of words, a resignation in the light of the impossibility of creating a simulacrum or a congener in stories which will be the Incarnation of the Unnamable, the voice becomes more frenzied, the punctuation by comma more insistent, the mind's connected logic going to be replaced by short stabs of expression. Anxiety builds up, desperation sets in and the desire to escape from this condition of words intolerable, yet tolerable:

I'll never stir, never speak, they'd never go silent, never depart, they'll never catch me, never stop trying, that's that. I'm listening. Well I prefer that, I must say I prefer that, that what, oh you know, who you, oh I suppose the audience, well well, so there's an audience, it's a public show, you buy your seat and you wait . . . you hear a voice, perhaps it's a recitation, that's the show, someone reciting, selected passages, old favourites, a poetry matinée, or someone improvising, you can hardly hear him . . . that's the show, free, gratis and for nothing, waiting alone, blind, deaf, you don't know where, you don't know for what, for a hand to come and draw you away, somewhere else, where perhaps it's worse. (p. 385)

The Unnamable is on the run from himself to himself, but he doesn't exist, cannot exist, exists. All that exists are words, stories, which 'he' is, which are 'he':

I'm all these words, all these strangers, this dust of words, with no ground for their settling, no sky for their dispersing, coming together to say, fleeing one another to say, that I am they, all of them . . . (p. 390)

But the words also say

that I'm something quite different, a quite different thing, a wordless thing in an empty place, a hard shut dry cold black place, where nothing stirs, nothing speaks, and that I listen and that I seek, like a caged beast born of caged beasts born of caged beasts . . . (ibid.)

But that which is not word cannot be said, that which is in words is not 'I'. The attempt to tell the story of 'I' is 'unimaginable, unspeakable', but 'that doesn't matter, the attempt must be made' (p. 417). And here one is at the heart of the mystery, that of having to write, with nothing to write with and nothing to write about. The work which dramatises the failure of fiction is a work which triumphantly succeeds in holding the reader's attention riveted to words, to the whole set of problems about fictional creation, the paradox of saying the unsayable or of saying what you say is unsayable. If the Unnamable is the one whose existence was always foreshadowed by the early heroes like Malone and Murphy, inconceivable and untouched by the bodied fictions they were, the Unnamable's essence cannot be other than individuated by fictional matter. And here we are confronted with Essence resisting Existence and being forced to go on with the impossible task of searching for itself:

... you must go on, I can't go on, you must go on, I'll go on, you must say words, as long as there are any, until they find me, until they say me, strange pain, strange sin, you must go on, perhaps it's done already, perhaps they have said me already, perhaps they have carried me to the threshold of my story, before the door that opens on my story, that would surprise me, if it opens, it will be I, it will be the silence, where I am, I don't know, I'll never know, in the silence you don't know, you must go on, I can't go on, I'll go on. (p. 418)

3

THEATRE OF SUFFERING

Beckett's work in the theatre starts before *Waiting for Godot* with an early unpublished play, *Eleutheria*, and a long study of the theatre (his friend, Professor Jean-Jacques Mayoux, told me of the many postcards received from Beckett urging him to attend this or that performance which was worthy of support).

His published work for the theatre shows the same overall pattern of the rest of his work in that it starts by calling in question the accepted idea of a play and then follows the path of diminution. The scale runs from the two-act play *Waiting for Godot* and then into one-act plays which grow smaller and smaller, with less and less action, until the latest 'dramaticule', *Breath*, which has no protagonist but a heap of junk for the centre of the stage, lights which dim and a sound of breath inhaled, held, exhaled and a birth-death cry.

His dramatic media include radio and television (and a single film, *Film*, with Buster Keaton) and his excursions into these have shown one remarkable quality. He has tried to examine and comprehend the peculiar properties of each medium and then to turn the medium into his vision, not translating this special vision into the new medium. This fact gives his radio pieces special interest, and his television play, *Eh Joe*, is an almost unique example of turning the camera to real account in the play.

But whatever medium of drama Beckett has worked in the resulting creation has that characteristic density, spareness and desolation which one comes to associate with all his work.

Waiting for Godot

Brendan Behan's claim that his theatre was for entertainment and Beckett's for lectures might be the truth if truth were as limited as that. In *Waiting for Godot* an audience is entertained but at a cost. The jokes are so terrible that they can't face telling them; the cross-talk peters out. The prat-falls are accidental and bad; they are circus clown routines managed in incompetent and uncaring ways.

But the two entertainers are more than this, or to put it more exactly, they are forced to the roles of entertainers and really they belonged to other worlds, social and cultural. Now they exist outside society and outside any considerations other than the basic ones of food, boots, getting from this day to the next, waiting for that something to happen which will change everything, which somehow will make a meaning in their meaningless world. But they, like we, reckon without the full implication of the held assertion that 'all is meaningless'. We take this, perhaps, to be an autobiographical statement really translatable by 'I can find no meaning in my life and in my world'. Others behave as though there was a purpose, a meaning, in their lives. They have created a meaning in their work, in their family, in their busy occupations in our bustling world. But our heroes have, for reasons unknown, no-thing of all this, but they are the raw substance so commonly dressed up in accidents of occupation, role, relationship. They are unaccom-modated men. Space and time find them, though space is empty, save for a mound and a tree; and time is no longer the measure of motion but an arbitrary imposition through which men crawl to a death they can never know.

Of course, stasis and silence are the conditions to which they fruit-lessly aspire, and, meantime, they do not need to employ their time to their advantage, because they have only disadvantage; but they have somehow or other to pass the time (though whatever devices they have for this purpose are futile because time would pass anyway, as they know very well). So, Vladimir—eastern European name—and Estragon—French Tarragon which flavours vinegar, soured wine—share circus clown's garb of big boots, capacious pockets, everlasting hand-me-down clothing, and the diminished respectability and gen-tility of bowler hats in a no-man's-land of despair and emptiness.

They carry impedimenta from a dead world, the dead world of a largely forgotten Christianity, the dead world of romantic love, the dead world of learning. Carrying this burden of dead voices they bear a largely inert mythology about them, and their relationship with, say, Christianity must be carefully recorded and seen for what it is. Certainly, Christianity is a religion of hope, based on the paradox of a Christ, Man-God, whose life was suffering and whose death un-deserved and that of a criminal. The suffering Christ is a strong attraction for the heroes, but He had the easier role:

Vladimir: But where he was it was warm, it was dry!
Estragon: Yes. And they crucified quick.

(p. 52)

All his life Estragon has compared himself to the crucified Christ, and Vladimir caresses the Augustinian sentence, as does Beckett, about the two thieves:

I am interested in the shape of ideas, even if I do not believe in them. There is a wonderful sentence in Augustine: I wish I could remember the Latin. It is even finer in Latin than in English. 'Do not despair; one of the thieves was saved. Do not presume; one of the thieves was damned.' That sentence has a wonderful shape. It is the shape that matters. (Beckett to Harold Hobson.[1] Quoted by Hugh Kenner in *Samuel Beckett: A Critical Study*, London, John Calder, 1962, p. 100.)

But the beauty of Beckett's apprehension of a balance which holds presumption and despair in balance around the concept of hope is not enough for *Waiting for Godot*. If one were to say that there is an even chance of salvation or damnation, given the two thieves' story, then the formula is further reduced in efficacy when, out of the four report-ers on the life of Christ, only two say anything about the thieves, and then only one of these two tells the story which everyone believes. People, the suggestion goes, are willing to believe what seems to them to offer some hope, against all the odds, then clutch at theological straws and make them the foundation of their lives. People are 'bloody ignorant apes' (or, more offensively, 'les gens sont des cons').

Let this discussion take place against a parody of the Japanese Noh plays' pine-tree, symbol of everlasting life, and a mound which is of unstated symbolic significance, and there are enough cross-references, suggestions and allusions for any poetic drama. The tree, really an artificial tree, a pantomime tree, can feed many suggestions. It is 'a weeping willow' as in *Hamlet*, 'Tit Willow' and 'Hang my harp on a weeping willow tree'. It is the 'tree of life', only in the sense that it is

1. The *Sunday Times* drama critic.

the tree of 'non-suicide'. It is the miracle of the spring visibly uttered
in a sterile landscape (though the French 'couvert de feuilles' is too
excessive and too clearly shouts *miracle*, and is reduced to 'four or five
leaves' in the translation into English). With the mound nearby, it
seems right to suggest, as a critic must in order to be true to his calling,
the empty cross and the closed tomb, a departed, absent or simply dead
Christ. So, there are enough hints and allusions to trap the unwary
critic who takes it as his function to make sense of the art-object, to
see structures, order, controlling motifs and reasons. And when we
come to the problem of 'doing the tree', as Alan Schneider did in his
production of the play, we need to be informed, as he was in his puzzle
by Beckett himself, that the tree is a Yoga position used as a prayerful
invocatory stance (which, by the play's definition, cannot even be
successfully performed, let alone set on foot a train of metaphysical or
psychological events).

Any myth that is generated by the play will do so at the expense of
and from the fragments of other ineffectual mythologies, and symbols
will be of doubtful value and status. The Christian will want it his way
and will want the play to belong to a demonstration of anguish at the
Death of God, a play which sees the despair of a Godless world and
which all the more clearly demonstrates the need man has for God in
his world, in his life. Beckett has allowed for this and inoculated his
play against it, and, like Watt, it looks as though it was put on a course
of injections of sterile pus. 'Godot' is obviously formed on 'God', but
what real connexion with God is very unsure indeed. Perhaps, like
Molloy's Mag where the 'g' spits on the 'Ma', the '-ot' spits on the
'God'

And I called her Mag because for me, without my knowing why, the letter g
abolished the syllable Ma, and as it were spat on it, better than any other
letter would have done. And at the same time I satisfied a deep and doubtless
unacknowledged need, the need to have a Ma, that is a mother, and to proclaim it, audibly. (*Molloy*, p. 17)

The public proclamation of the need for God (spat on), my kind of
God, as Molloy's is for Mother, my kind of mother, however senile,
blind and deaf, with confused and broken mind, is acknowledged, but
the response to the proclamation is savagely comic. Monsieur Godot
exists, but what they know about him adds up to 'an important person'
whose importance they invent (in order to get to this appointment
with them he will have to arrange his affairs, consult his bank-manager

and so on) and who will come 'tomorrow'. He has an evangelist, the
good-news bringer, a little boy (Middle English *evangel* could mean
'youth', 'young man') and he appears twice, or, at least, the French
text says it is the same boy who appears in both acts. This small boy
can give the good-news, but to Monsieur Albert. But, is this Vladimir's
real surname; or is it his real Christian name; or is it someone else's
name and Vladimir is receiving someone else's message? And the boy
can give information which seems confirmatory of Monsieur Godot as
an Old Testament Jehovah, long white beard and vile temper. He beats
the sheep-minder but not his brother the goat-herd, a reversal of the
sheep and goats separation by the Last Judgment, and he is a pastoral
figure. But we must note that the boy is a liar; he has been waiting, in
the second Act, for Pozzo and Lucky to depart before he enters (as any
actor must wait in the wings for his entrance) and he is afraid. Like any
peasant he only wishes to placate and satisfy the moods of his interro-
gators, and his information is as suspect as the peasant who sees your
tired shoulders and sweating face and tells you, when asked, that 'It's
just a step to Bally'. He knows that you have five or more miles of
aching tramp ahead, but who is he to dishearten you? So, Monsieur
Godot's archetypal appearance is guaranteed only in so far as the boy
gives the answers expected by his interrogator.

All positive indications are balanced by contra-indications. We,
unsuspecting, see the grotesque bourgeois Pozzo arrive, triumphantly
whipping on Lucky, who is tethered by his neck and burdened with
Pozzo's multifarious travelling equipment. So we read the signs of
social order, oppression, the slavery of the working class, exploitation,
inhumanity. Pozzo, landowner, self-satisfied, brutal and cultivated man
of leisure with his rhetoric, throat-spray, Peterson pipe, gold half-
hunter with dead-beat escapement, is so clearly signalled to us that we
are thrown off balance when the situation begins more elaborately to
unfold. Lucky, ironic name, is not a chattel merely. He is a walking
vade-mecum, the equivalent of the little copy of Aeschylus, Horace or
Byron in the pocket of a traveller from an earlier century. He is the
former tutor, instructor and mine of information whose mind has been
used like a gramophone record by Pozzo. Now the mind has broken
down and the double suggestion is that age and long use has worn it
out as have the kinds of intellectual concern which have most engaged
it. And, naturally, the stones among which this machine has laboured
are those insoluble nonsense puzzles of theology: God's nature, un-

utterable, ineffable, compounded in negatives by the mind (athambia, aphasia); the punishment which seems arbitrary, unmerited and for reasons unknown, the necessary decline of man towards death, towards Golgotha, towards the sea's shore (Normandy or Connemara); the irrational curve of a man's life, a man's mind. Given these constants the mind which tries to understand, elucidate or comprehend must crack, must be destroyed. To try to express the inexpressible, the un-utterable or the ineffable, 'to utter or to eff it', is 'doomed to failure, doomed, doomed to failure' (*Watt*, p. 61). To take the terms of the speech as indicative of more than a hopeless mind chasing an insoluble puzzle is to invite critical disaster.

Furthermore, the second act shows a rapidity of deterioration already demonstrated as a fact in the first. There Pozzo had successively mislaid his atomizer, his pipe and his watch. Things are falling away, and, when he reappears, he is blind, has not driven Lucky to market as he announced in Act I, but has shortened the rope so that Lucky, now dumb, is leading him rather than being driven on by the whip. These two are now bound together but in a less obviously socially critical manner. What suggestions had been laid down in the audience's mind are rescinded, negated, and a more meaningless relationship has been established. They have moved closer to the sort of complementary interdependence which has no obviousness, no simple rational explanation, which Vladimir and Estragon have already shown. There, one stinks from his mouth, the other from his feet; one is more nearly masculine in his kind of mind, solicitous for the welfare of the weaker, more emotional partner; the other more nearly feminine in tantrums, and has a decayed poetic mind. Vladimir is the provider with the store of turnips and carrots, the parody of husband; Estragon is the one who needs to be guided and sustained. They form a parodic marriage bond, and they are sexless, though they could have formed an elegant homo-sexual love-match ending their lives in a mutual suicide by leaping hand-in-hand from the Eiffel Tower in the 'nineties ('But they wouldn't even let us up now'), and they might achieve a similar love-death romantic ending ('To cease upon the midnight with no pain, Whilst thou art pouring forth thy soul abroad in such an ecstasy') in the final erection and emission in hanging themselves from the tree (which is impossible). As we come to recognise with increasing clarity, Beckett's economy lies in giving the mind just enough of a suggestion to create a working meaning, but any more would be excess. Similarly, when it becomes clear that Vladimir and Estragon have been established as the diminished remnant of Man, and therefore our representatives, they are made to declare themselves reluctant representatives of mankind. It is thus made clear to us that we need to witness stage-heroes as our representatives, but that all that Beckett can offer us is this pair of defective moribunds dragooned by the author into a role they know they are incapable of fulfilling adequately. The play, because it is a play, works by arousing traditional responses in the audience, but when it sees the protagonists openly disavowing themselves from the roles assigned them by the author, whilst still conventionally fulfilling them, the play's ironies deepen.

The audience has been accustomed to a play's having an action as well as a plot, possibly proceeding according to Aristotelian rules about protasis, discovery, climax and resolution, or to having a story unfolded in several acts. What it is not prepared for is a 'drama stripped for inaction', for a two-act play which displays the same basic 'events' in both acts, but showing in its second series an accelerated state of decay. When the programme, or the text, announces 'The next day' for the second act, we take the words literally (as we do in 'Three Months Later'). But what kind of 'next day' is it when leaves have suddenly come on the tree, when Pozzo has gone blind 'one day, when does it matter?' and when Estragon's boots seem to have altered? The answer is that all days are identical, all exist in a repetitious chain, and mirror or parody one another. Any two days, chosen at random at whatever interval from an infinite series, or a series which ends with 'the last day' after which there is no 'next day', will do to show the series for what it is. All events xyz will have analogous $x_1y_1z_1 \cdots x_ny_nz_n$, and this is absurd. The day of Act I ends, as does the day of Act II, with 'Let's go'. *They do not go.* Yet Act II can start; Vladimir and Estragon have gone and returned (contrary to the stage-directions), and the conclusion in which nothing is concluded points, against the stage-direction and against all the odds, towards 'the next day', *ad infinitum*. The circular song of Act II's beginning has been in Beckett's mind (appearing in *The Unnamable*, p. 382), and its terrible beauty *is* that there is no place to stop; once you start it must proceed into infinite circularity, yet you stop. As Beckett said that only fatigue and disgust prevented the incorporation of the *Addenda* to *Watt* in the body of the novel, so only fatigue and disgust prevent us from going on with the interminable.

Endgame

Having terminated the interminable dramatic world of *Waiting for Godot* with its wanderers of no fixed abode, Beckett turned the attention of his readers to his fiction. Then, five years after the appearance of *En Attendant Godot* in 1952, *Fin de Partie* was published in 1957, to be translated and issued the following year as *Endgame*.

From the bleak expanse of the empty road to nowhere of the previous play, and from the contrasting worlds of the static figures of Vladimir and Estragon and the dynamically retarding Pozzo and Lucky, we are fixed in the last abode. Instead of *Waiting for Godot* to end, endlessly, we are waiting for the end, 'finished, almost finished'.

This play operates from a complex mode of dead metaphors, bringing a variety of symbols together which mutually frustrate each other and themselves. 'Endgame' is the final movement of a game of chess, the board cleaned of all but a few pieces, one of which is King; but in this play we have only one of the two colours ('very red face' for both Clov and Hamm) for the protagonists, only one side of the board. The metaphor of the chess-game is so far frustrated, broken-backed, and any critical attempt to pursue too closely the moves of the play in chess terms will be equally frustrating.

Again, the world of Genesis called up by Hamm's name and the desolation of the earth outside the shelter which is the little world of Hamm will only operate partially as metaphor. If Hamm is Ham, son of Noe, then Nagg will be Noe, but he is not. None the less, we do feel the resonance of the simple Genesis story in vi. 9–13:

9. This is the story of Noe. Noe was a just man, blameless among the men of his day.
10. He walked with God. Noe became the father of three sons, Sem, Ham and Japheth.
11. The earth was corrupt in the sight of God, and it was filled with violence.
12. God saw that the earth was corrupt; for all men lived corruptly on the earth.
13. And God said to Noe, 'The end of all creatures of flesh is in my mind; the earth is full of violence because of them. I will destroy them with the earth'.

We feel that violence and corruption and 'the end of all creatures of flesh' is in our minds in the play, but we cannot feel it in the Genesis manner. What we see is that Hamm is terrified lest the earth renew

itself again, lest the flea, which Clov claims to have, start the whole
evolutionary cycle all over again:

Clov: (*anguished, scratching himself*). I have a flea!
Hamm: A flea! Are there still fleas?
Clov: On me there's one. (*Scratching.*) Unless it's a crablouse.
Hamm: (*Very perturbed.*) But humanity might start from there all over
            again! Catch him, for the love of God!   (p. 27)

Noe's rescue work for the renewal of life exists as ironic counterpoint
with Beckett's play, and the moral corruption of God's creation which
offended Him in Genesis converts into the play's anger at the corpse-
smell of the universe:

Hamm: Yes, but how would I know, if you were merely dead in your
            kitchen?
Clov: Well . . . sooner or later I'd start to stink.
Hamm: You stink already. The whole place stinks of corpses.
Clov: The whole universe.
Hamm: (*angrily*). To hell with the universe!   (p. 33)

God's anger and omnipotence, restrained for the 'just man', Noe, again
ironically counters Hamm's impotent rage, and his assumption of
tyrannical behaviour. But he is an impotent tyrant and we are clear
about the limitations of his power.

  The whole play is set in motion by Clov, not by Hamm, and Clov's
removal of the 'old sheet' from the two ashbins and from Hamm in his
armchair has no single assignable significance. As so often with Beckett,
the possible explanations are too many: perhaps this routine is the
routine of any morning, and the analogy is the removal of the covering
from the canary's cage; but perhaps this is an occasional enactment,
long delayed and repeatable *ad infinitum*, and the analogy is the return
from long absence to the country home and the removal of the dust-
sheets from the furniture. Whatever the analogy, we are certainly right
in supposing that the world's behaviour is not mirrored on the stage,
but that the stage comments savagely on man's condition and his
desire to make a self-important tragedy out of his deliquescent existence, to see himself as having played his best for a loss not a win. The
play will not allow Hamm, blind King, to see himself defeated, nor will
it allow him to act himself into a position where all is lost. For the play
to do what Hamm wants—defeat and isolation—then his final soliloquy discarding people, toy, whistle ought to be a *soliloquy*. But it is
no such thing, whatever Hamm acts it as. He asks the absent Clov for

the last favour of being covered with the sheet, and, thinking this last request refused, he winds himself up for his 'Old endgame lost of old, play and lose and have done with losing'. But Clov, impassive and motionless, has his eyes fixed on Hamm for the great last perform-ance, wrecking the soliloquy and giving an audience for Hamm's con-clusion to his story-telling and an ironic twist to Hamm's last words addressed to his handkerchief, his 'old stancher', 'You . . . remain'.

However, though the performance by the master is ruined in this respect, Hamm is perfectly aware that it is all a game, but what game is unclear from the contradictory allusions. Hamm uses the tennis 'Deuce', one point to each opponent and start again, after the raising and resumption of 'his hat':

Raise hat. (*He raises his toque.*) Peace to our . . . arses. (*Pause.*) And put on again. (*He puts on his toque.*) Deuce. (p. 52)

This is followed by a reference to 'calling' which might be the response to 'heads or tails' or to the bid in a card-game ('Misère' or 'Five No Trumps'):

A few more squirms like that and I'll call. (ibid.)

Behind all these metaphors in the play lie precise allusions to suffer-ing both in the Old and New Testaments which are introduced by the opening words of Clov and Hamm. 'Finished, it's finished, nearly finished it must be nearly finished' (p. 12) seem clearly enough to be a distorted echo of Christ's *Consummatum Est* on the cross, while Hamm's 'Can there be misery—(*he yawns*)—loftier than mine? No doubt. Formerly' (p. 12) seem to echo the *Lamentations of Jeremiah* (a type of Christ):

O all ye that pass by the way, attend, and see if there be any sorrow like to my sorrow: for he hath made a vintage of me, as the Lord spoke in the day of his fierce anger. (1.12)

But, lest we walk in the steps of the unwary collator of cross-references and judge the play as though it were Christian, we are presented, two-thirds of the way through the play, with the attempt to pray to God. Of course, there is no divine intervention; and so Hamm explodes:

'The bastard! He doesn't exist!'

only to be qualified, however gnomically, by Clov's

'Not yet.' (p. 38)
    D

Now we see something about the way Beckett uses metaphors and images, well known and a currency in the culture, but useful only within heavy qualifications and strict boundaries.

When one locates the play within a set which has often been likened to the inside of a skull, with its grey light and its two small windows high up right and left, ingenuity runs riot. We can, if we so wish, see Hamm as mind and Clov as decrepit senses, clown-like in his stiff staggering walk and constant forgetfulness of the things which he should have so easily by rote. We can, also, if we so wish, see the Freudian principles of Ego, Id, Super Ego at work. We can see just as much as we wish because Beckett has not closed the boundaries here, has not made reference and allusions clear for the critical ferret. Headaches are there for the asking, but Beckett reminds us that we must provide our own aspirin.

We both have and do not have enough intellectual equipment to understand the situation being enacted for us on stage until we recognise that Hamm in his castored armchair and his controller-servant Clov are *not* a master and servant whose analogues we could find in ordinary life; they are kept together by something which is incomprehensible.

Clov: So you all want me to leave you.
Hamm: Naturally.
Clov: Then I'll leave you.
Hamm: You can't leave us.
Clov: Then I shan't leave you.
    Pause.
Hamm: Why don't you finish us? (*Pause.*) I'll tell you the combination of
    the larder if you promise to finish me.
Clov: I couldn't finish you.
Hamm: Then you shan't finish me.   (p. 29)

All we know is that we are being helped, by Clov's setting all in motion, to a demonstration of the gradual ending, the near stasis of a corpsed universe and the few squirms before the end. We are confronted by a blind story-teller whose interminable story must finish only when he finishes; a *Malone Dies* man, whose invention and memory are in satisfactory working order for sufficient doling out of words which pass the time and help us to get on from one moment to the next. In this play he delights in an audience who will be made to appreciate the tale but who are really ignored for the primary satisfaction of the teller's enjoyment of his own skill at telling.

It was a glorious bright day, I remember, fifty by the heliometer, but already the sun was sinking down into the . . . down among the dead. (*Normal tone.*) Nicely put, that. (*Narrative tone.*) Come on now, come on, present your petition and let me resume my labours. (*Pause. Normal tone.*) There's English for you. Ah well . . . (p. 36)

So, this time the telling of the tale is also the actor's holding of attention, and Hamm joins Pozzo in a heightened rhetoric of delivery. But, where Pozzo enjoyed his sunset declamation and held his audience spell-bound, Hamm isn't allowed his sweet glory unalloyed.

Hamm: Then let it end! (*Clov goes toward ladder.*) With a bang! (*Clov gets up on ladder, gets down again, looks for telescope, sees, it, picks it up, gets up ladder, raises telescope.*) Of Darkness! And me? Did anyone ever have pity on me?
Clov: (*lowering the telescope, turning towards Hamm.*) What? (*Pause.*) Is it me you're referring to?
Hamm: (*Angrily.*) An aside, ape! Did you never hear an aside before? (*Pause.*) I'm warming up for my last soliloquy.

(p. 49)

The actor hams, and the self-conscious artifice is part of the ending of the game; all games must end in a draw. So the final 'soliloquy' is not the last move in the game, though it is the last move for the moment. Hamm not only 'plays' his part but he insists on maintaining before us the nature of the play as 'play' ('More complications! . . . not an under-plot, I trust', ibid.), and we become conscious that Hamm wants to be the one who structures and plans the moves in this final performance. He even sees himself as an ironic Prospero dismissing Nagg with 'Our revels now are ended' (p. 39). Unfortunately for him, he has to play within circumstances already established of everything running down (no more painkiller, Nagg and Nell 'bottled', Mother Pegg 'extin-guished') and can only enact his endless story and wait for Clov to go and then 'speak no more'.

Clov, too, is playing the game as well as he can, sees the end as the thing which comes but which he cannot understand, and one feels his kinship with Watt, another servant, in an incomprehensible service who leaves, again without understanding. But Clov is not Watt. Like Watt's words Clov's lose their meaning:

I ask the words that remain—sleeping, waking, morning, evening. They have nothing to say. (p. 151)

But his speech, his curtain speech, isn't his own speech; it is provoked, as Lucky's is, by order from the master: 'A few words . . . from your heart' (p. 50). It is, therefore, a prepared speech, dismissable as 'theatre', or as a representative speech of the departing guest, a Beckettian *Nunc Dimittis Domine*. So, while linking Clov with Watt, it represents the exit from life in the light where one has grown old in a prison, and where the body has shrunk and then disintegrated into dust, dust back to dust.

> I open the door of the cell and go. I am so bowed I only see the feet, if I open my eyes, and between my legs a little trail of black dust. I say to myself that the earth is extinguished, though I never saw it lit. (p. 51)

But, even if Clov is to go, unaccountably and with no single assignable reason, the rest may be silence but not, unfortunately, utter emptiness. From our experience of *The Unnamable* we can guess that the fate which Hamm predicts for Clov will be Hamm's when this 'Endplay' is ended. The last move may be Hamm's reassuming his sudarium, his uncomforting comforter ('You . . . remain'), but we remember the prediction:

> Infinite emptiness will be all around you, all the resurrected dead of all the ages wouldn't fill it, and there you'd be like a little bit of grit in the middle of the steppe. (*Pause.*) Yes, one day you'll know what it is, you'd be like me, except that you won't have anyone with you, because you won't have pity on anyone because there won't be anyone left to have pity on. (pp. 28–9)

Hamm has played and lost, but he will go on surrounded by emptiness which he, like the Unnamable, will have to people as he can. Of course, Clov may not go, or he may go and come back, and the moves will be inaugurated again, with the board cleared of all pieces but two. But all we know is that Clov does not go, and that the King, so desirous of being a tyrant, sits impotent in his chair, things having run down, if not out.

The play never reveals what exists 'outside', though it is death outside, and, teasingly, Clov almost introduces Hamm's dreaded 'complications' of a 'sub-plot' by spotting a small boy. Beckett presumably thought that the French original *Fin de Partie* was too open to specific Biblical interpretation and reduced the status of the boy as seen by Clov. Originally reference to Moses might have indicated a mock-salvation, and the possibility that Clov is deceiving Hamm is firmly implanted. Now, though that possibility is open, the boy's existence for Hamm is no problem:

'If he exists he'd die there or he'd come here. And if he doesn't . . .' (p. 50)

He is neither a threat nor a promise, and no more is needed of Clov. The sighting is Clov's and he is either inventing or he's not. If he's inventing he must have a reason. His reason must be either to frighten, enliven or encourage Hamm. He wants to see the boy as a threat to the renewal of the world, analogous to his flea (though small boys can only procreate with a suitable partner, and none exists in *this* world). Hamm cannot be threatened in this way, and Clov's usefulness is ended, the last possible move to keep his place, to hurt or enliven Hamm. If he is not inventing then the impossible conditions within and without will take care of the boy, and again nothing can happen to stop the ending.

And in this bitter attack on the world of sustaining toys, palliatives and useless restoratives, the play demonstrates cruelty, absurd misery and a violent antipathy to answers to the question about the meaning of man's existence. We play the game in order to lose and we live in a world which forms the joke Nagg tells, and Nell's observation that 'Nothing is funnier than unhappiness, I grant you that' (p. 20). The play is one of suffering and anguish in a dying world, a theatrical assault on the audience who come to be entertained by characters who hope against hope that 'We're not beginning to . . . to . . . mean something' (p. 27). The uneasy audience is not simply accepted as the necessary convention but as the part of the play which must remember its part. We are part of the charade and planned for. Clov climbs his lookout's ladder and lets fall his telescope:

I did it on purpose. (*He gets down, picks up the telescope, turns it on the auditorium.*) I see . . . a multitude . . . in transports . . . of joy. (*Pause.*) That's what I call a magnifier. (*He lowers the telescope, turns towards Hamm.*) Well? Don't we laugh? (p. 25)

We do not. Because we try to make sense of the play and want, like Clov, a world of order, we are deliberately led and misled by the play, given too many meanings or none. The effect is the same; incomprehension. Why should Nagg and Nell have white faces? We seem to have the other chess colour and to have the King and Queen of the opposing side; and their impossibility of moving, having lost their legs in a tandem crash, and now retained in dustbins, would make this a very unequal game. But Beckett, when questioned, merely indicated that the faces are white for contrast. We can make no sense of it, and to tidy it all up by exegesis would be both absurd and wrong. All we can say is that, in the end, man's role is absurd and meaningless in a world designed for cruelty, though agonisingly one can recognise the possible beauty too:

Look! There! All that rising corn! And there! Look! The sails of the herring fleet! All that loveliness! (*Pause.*) He'd snatch away his hand and go back into his corner. Appalled, All he had seen was ashes. (*Pause.*) He alone had been spared. (*Pause.*) Forgotten. (p. 32)

But the man in Hamm's little story was accounted mad, and, by telling it of a madman whose 'case is . . . was not so . . . so unusual', Hamm disallows the possibility of treating him as mad, but allows the possibility for this unusual view to be one shared by many. In Hamm's way we are shown the world of ashes and witness the terror and comic anguish of figures who suffer inanities and desolation, in the world as corpsed.

Krapp's Last Tape

A tapeworm is only excreted completely from the intestine at the cost of starvation and a massive dose of some substance which is most unpleasant to the worm. Normally, without dosing only fragments of it are excreted.

The thought of a tapeworm as long as a cricket pitch living secretly in the stomach of a film star, or a beetle quietly chewing the feet of a close-sitting hen arouses in us a feeling of macabre amusement. (*Fleas, Flukes and Cuckoos: A Study of Bird Parasites*, Miriam Rothschild and Theresa Clay, Grey Arrow edition, 1961, p. 16.)

It would take a massive dose of something very unpleasant to finish Krapp's tape.

Krapp's Last Tape is organised around memory in several senses. An artist has substituted a comprehensive mechanical tape-recorder for the more conventional notebook or journal of earlier centuries. And this, incidentally, pushed Krapp into a future time beyond our present which is made explicit by the stage-direction 'A late evening in the future'. But no concession is made to time; the artist is, as ever, forlorn, ageless as a clown with a 'surprising pair of dirty white boots, size ten at least, very narrow and pointed', and a white face and purple nose. 'Macabre amusement.' He is, as ever, falling into decrepitude and his senses failing. But his past voice and past experiences are still not on the tapes, and all is organised with the precision of a ledger which is the master of all the memories. The moment chosen for the first mechanical memory is the recording made thirty years ago on the artist's thirty-ninth birthday, and this night again is the occasion of a yearly entry. Even at thirty-nine he had been indulging his tapes with 'new retrospects', but each new retrospect, so the logic would run, would project new hopes, a more genuinely satisfying 'old eye' over the past and would record the increase in vision. The pathos is that this series of yearly retrospects and projections ends in the denial of the 'vision', of the 'great fire' which the climacteric thirty-ninth birthday recording shows. The love-affair which stimulated the vision and the fire is, of course, long dead, though we would like very much to have the full expression of the vision which Krapp impatiently rushes past in his search for the expression of the moment of romantic stasis where love is full but not yet spent, where the erotic is stilled and entranced in a natural lakeside cul-de-sac. The recording is probably of the end of the affair, but is presenting a moment of dreamy calm, with no passion, only a gentle rhythmic dance of erotic peace.

The present Krapp can only snarl his rejection of his former self, but he is drawn back into his 'old misery'. 'Once wasn't enough for you.' To be drawn back into the past, into that immediacy of the recorded vigour and the arrogant rejection of that love, of the voice so confident in its control of verbal rhythms, of its conceit with its own power, is to recognise the falsity of the fire of the artistic imagination which was going to be the source and basis of the success in the future. The past Krapp can say:

Perhaps my best years are gone. When there was a chance of happiness. But I wouldn't want them back. Not with the fire in me now. No, I wouldn't want them back.

but the present Krapp has no fire left. His artist's success is recorded on his sixty-ninth birthday as 'seventeen copies old, of which eleven at trade price to free circulating libraries beyond the seas. Getting known. (*Pause.*) One pound six and something, eight I have little doubt'.

What remains is Krapp. The addiction to bananas, to drink, to retrospects, to his mechanical memory and hope recorder. He hasn't changed, though his moments are all tedium now ('Revelled in the word spool (*with relish*). Spoool! Happiest moment of the past half million'). Then his year's record was symbolic enough to satisfy any artist. The year of his mother's eventual death, the lighting up of a year of profound spiritual gloom and indigence by a 'memorable night in March' when the vision came. This parody of Stephen Dedalus's vision in *A Portrait of the Artist as a Young Man* should bring us closer to the recognition of Krapp as the artist as an old man. In fact, Joyce can afford to mock Stephen in *Portrait*, and, to some extent, in *Ulysses*, as he, Joyce/Stephen, is now writing. The artist has proven himself by writing the work in which he appears as so callow and *ingénu*. This artist, Krapp, is disproving himself as an artist and he is on his 'last tape'. There are no more tapes in the drawer, so the title proclaims; and we arrive at a *terminus ad quem* from a *terminus a quo*, rather than write from a *terminus ad quem* back to a *terminus a quo*.

As if that isn't bad enough, Beckett makes it quite clear at the end that a second kind of memory is involved in Krapp which is entirely at odds with the specificity of time, place and voice of the tapes in the long tapeworm. This is the comforting fantasy-memory without the specificity of those recording moments; this is the 'wandering' of the mind of the Krapp propped up in the dark:

Be again in the dingle on a Christmas Eve, gathering holly, the red-berried. (*Pause.*) Be again on Croghan on a Sunday morning, in the haze, with the bitch, stop and listen to the bells. (*Pause.*)

There is no specific moment involved; there is no one occasion remembered, but an imaginative construction made out of times past, long past, used as a consolatory fantasy. The times are those before maturity; pre-sexual, and pre-artistic. These moments of boyhood peace and excitement, times full of promise (Christmas Eve not Christmas Day, Sunday morning not Sunday evening), are the constructed fantasies of 'being again'.

We have parody Proust, Krapp rummaging *à la recherche du temps perdu*, and finding no blinding clarity of involuntary memory. The artist signally fails, and the mechanical memory fails, and Krapp can only gather imaginary fragments to hug himself warm while he lies propped up in the dark.

RADIO DRAMA

All That Fall

A commissioned radio play for the BBC Third Programme, first broadcast in 1957, shows Beckett's concern with the vehicle of sound for drama and his attempt to orchestrate voices and noises into a poetic whole. The question of the insidious hold that poetic drama has on the mind of the creative dramatist is brought into mind, and the whole range of dangers which the need to make drama 'poetic' again in our time has meant. T. S. Eliot's struggle with the idea of 'poetic' in 'poetic drama' has dictated much critical thought and debate, and Beckett is obviously aware acutely of the problems. He is a poet and nothing that he handles is other than a poetry of denudement, a poetry of the minimal affirmation.

It is plain that Beckett knows of the audience's expectations which have been built up by the convention of the play for radio. The listener is encouraged to use his imagination, aided by the careful deployment of sounds by sound engineers to fill his mind with the *mise en scène*, the atmospherics, the backcloth of sounds against which voices (the equivalents of people) will move. So, the pastoral nature of a play set in the country will be introduced by representative country sounds gradually faded down to allow human voices (the protagonists of action) to be faded up on the recording machine. Burlesque treatment will make us aware of the 'noises off', make us ironically witness the mechanisms and contrivances of horses' hooves as coconut shells, and so on.

Beckett's treatment depends on using the convention of the introduction by pastoral noises but making us aware of the artificiality and contrivance of the noises by having human imitations of 'rural sounds'. The result is not simply burlesque but a parody of an orchestra taking the note from the first violin and then all playing the note together for the satisfaction of the conductor. Then the 'pastoral symphony' can start. And music in several ways is involved in this 'symphony'. Maddy Rooney listens, as we do, to the '*Music faint from house by way.* "*Death and the Maiden*" '. An old woman's voice comments sadly on another 'Poor woman. All alone in that ruinous old house.' The mortal condition of life see-sawing nearer to death is brought out clearly. The romantic music (Schubert's Quartet no. 14 in D minor) involves the little world of the listener's present awareness in an ironic recognition of a complexity of suffering, beauty and isolation. A lone, shuffling woman and a world of decay is caught up in locomotion on an evolutionary scale, from Christy's hinny and cart, then Mr Tyler's bicycle to Mr Slocum's car, and on to the station and the railway-train. Each stage in this scale is a stage also up the social ladder, from the peasant to the 'retired bill-broker' to the Clerk of the Racecourse and the

D*

Station Master, his minions and Miss Fitt. But each stage presents its own piquancy. Christy and his hinny are left behind with the load of sty-dung still to be sold as the hinny refuses to move, and the other triumphant Christy of Synge's *Playboy of the Western World* is ironically alluded to. Mr Tyler's bicycle develops a flat rear tyre again and he rides off on the rim: 'You'll tear your tube to ribbons!' Mr Slocum's car refuses to start after he has switched off the engine to hoist Mrs Rooney into it:

All morning she went like a dream and now she is dead. That is what you get for a good deed. (p. 15)

All is running down, and Mrs Rooney is the centre from which we discover the extent of the decay, the general direction downwards that everything points towards:

Mr Slocum: May I offer you a lif[t], Mrs Rooney? Are you going in my direction?
Mrs Rooney: I am, Mr Slocum, we all are.   (p. 15)

Christy's wife and daughter are 'no better' and 'no worse'; Mr Tyler's 'poor daughter' has had an Irish rhetorical version of a pan-hysterectomy:

Mrs Rooney: What news of your poor daughter?
Mr Tyler: Fair, fair. They removed everything, you know, the whole . . . er . . . bag of tricks. Now I am grandchildless.   (p. 10)

Mr Slocum's mother is 'fairly comfortable':

Mr Slocum: We manage to keep her out of pain. That is the great thing, Mrs Rooney, is it not?
Mrs Rooney: Yes, indeed, Mr Slocum, that is the great thing, I don't know how you do it.

It is the women who seem to suffer most, females as the pathetic figures in the background, or the hen as the visible analogue of accidental but sudden death:

O, mother, you have squashed her, drive on, drive on. (*The car accelerates. Pause.*) What a death! One minute picking happy at the dung, on the road, in the sun, with now and then a dust bath, and then—bang—all her troubles over. (*Pause.*) All the laying and the hatching. (*Pause.*) Just one great squawk and then . . . peace. (*Pause.*) They would have slit her weasand in any case. (pp. 15–16)

Sympathetic enquiries by Mrs Rooney turn out to be perfunctory and not pursued; the stupidity of Mr Slocum's driving kills a hen, but that death is seen as a blessed release. People are kept going or people keep themselves going. Though sex is dead for Mrs Rooney, she keeps going. Romance still flickers in and around her. Ring-doves coo and immediately the triggered response from her is

Venus birds! Billing in the woods all the long summer long. (*Pause.*) Oh cursed corset! If I could let it out, without indecent exposure. Mr Tyler! Mr Tyler! Come back and unlace me behind the hedge! (*She laughs wildly,* ceases.) (p. 13)

But nothing lasts, and the sex is flickering sadly. Like Joyce's Bloom she is haunted by the memory of her dead child, and like Molly's half-rhyme child, Milly, Maddy's half-rhyme child is Minnie. And Minnie alive, now, would be Minnie running down like the rest:

Mrs Rooney: (*brokenly.*) In her forties now she'd be, I don't know, fifty girding up her lovely little loins, getting ready for the change . . . (p. 12)

Frustration, impotence and the comedy of rich absurdities in the Irish manner ('Wait, for God's sake, you'll have me beheaded'. 'Who's that crucifying his gearbox, Tommy') are all presented through the confrontation of Mrs Rooney and the circumambient human reality. And to this point in the sound play we feel we know the kind of work we are listening to, a soured comedy of ideas presented symbolically but through a materialistic medium; a particularisation of a general thesis that 'all life is short', a *lacrimae rerum*. But this is only the journey out to the station which will need the journey back to the beginning to round it out, a modification of the circular epic journey, a minimal Bloomsday. And, like Bloomsday, this day in the life and death of Maddy Rooney has a specificity which needs nothing. Unusually, for Beckett, we know the time of day, the day of the week and the time of year. Everything is past its mid-point. The day is past noon, the working week is finished (and we are left with the 'week-end') after the sixth month of the year. But, as Joyce's Bloomsday had a private set of significances for the writer and so was of magical importance, Beckett's has an obviously mathematical character, the fixed series, the finite allowance of hours in the day, days in the week, months in the year, and years in a life. The specificity is metaphoric, not simply naturalistic. Bloomsday has become Fadingday.

But we are deceived. The play is double, and what we are led to expect, a vehicle for a pessimistic presentation in a jocoserious manner of a view of life, a poetic drama, is only half of what Beckett gives us. The other half is the parody of the 'whodunnit'. The train is delayed because of an accident, or, as Mr Barrell puts it, 'All I know is there has been a hitch. All traffic is retarded' (p. 25). Interest is aroused, doused, re-illumined, and we await the train bearing Dan, Miss Fitt's mother and Mr Tyler's friend, Hardy, the preacher for the morrow on the text 'The Lord upholdeth all that fall and raiseth up all those that be bowed down'.

The second part of the play increases the concern about the train's delay, and gradually we come to recognise that something has happened which Dan Rooney wishes to keep from his wife. We learn from Jerry what it is when he runs panting to give Mr Rooney something that he had dropped:

It looks like a kind of ball. And yet it is not a ball. (p. 40)

Mr Rooney obviously knows something about the event as his groan when Jerry starts the devastating revelation tells us. The revelation itself is punishingly sharp and the hearer suffers a series of blows:

It was a little child fell out of the carriage, Ma'am. (*Pause.*) On to the line, Ma'am. (*Pause.*) Under the wheels, Ma'am. (p. 41)

Did Dan push the child from the carriage? Is the object a child's ball? Why does Dan keep his wife in the dark and distract her by a rhetorical performance equivalent to Hamm's in *Endgame*? These questions only point towards possibilities. There are no certainties other than the terrible ones revealed by Jerry, and there are no more words from either Maddy or Dan. We only hear their dragging steps and their halting to the rise and fall of the tempest of wind and rain. The rest is not silence after the tragedy, but the elemental fury and unconcern, and there are no solutions to the question, no neat tying of ends. Furthermore, whatever the results of the death on the lives of Maddy and Dan might be, all we can say is that they carry on. We have been led up to the death or murder and are left without a solution to 'whodunnit'. We have come back circuitously to the beginning of the play's start, but we are not completing a circular Vico road. The journey has taken time, and time has taken its toll.

'There is that lovely laburnum again' had come into Maddy's speech at the tail of a temporal sequence:

Love, that is all I asked, a little love, daily, twice daily, fifty years of twice daily love like a Paris horse-butcher's regular, what normal woman wants affection? A peck on the jaw at morning, near the ear, and another at evening, peck, peck, till you grow whiskers on you. There is that lovely laburnum again. (p. 9)

And, towards the end, the 'lovely laburnum' treads on the heels of another temporal sequence, but this time that of the rotting leaves in the ditch:

Mr Rooney: In June? Rotting leaves in June?
Mrs Rooney: Yes, dear, from last year, and from the year before last, and from the year before that again. (*Silence. Rainy Wind. They move on. Dragging steps, etc.*) There is that lovely laburnum again. Poor thing, it is losing all its tassels. (p. 37)

'All that fall': the rain falls; the laburnum tassels fall, and they combine in a 'Golden drizzle'.

Much has been lost on the journey, a discovery has been made which accounts for the loss of fifteen minutes in the schedule of the train from the city. The trivial acts involved in a painful progress to a suburban railway station by an old woman with heart and kidney trouble, 'destroyed with sorrow and pining and gentility and churchgoing and fat and rheumatism and childlessness' (p. 9), are redeemed from mindlessness by their organisation, their stark isolation from the background of sounds and by their symmetrical inevitability. The pastoral chorus leads to the crescendo and fury of the tempest of wind and rain, but no redemption in the symphony by movement back again to peace. The sounds take over from the voices; the sounds can always control the hearer's response to the voices. One example which needs some explanation is the way Maddy's voice is counterpointed by the 'noises off'. One can expect a voice to respond to sounds and comment on them because they *are* the external world for that voice. But what happens when the voice can call up the noises and create the external world?

Mrs Rooney: All is still. No living soul in sight. There is no one to ask. The world is feeding. The wind——(*brief wind*)——Scarcely stirs the leaves and the birds——(*brief chirps*)——are tired of of singing. The cows——(*brief moo*)——and sheep——(*brief baa*)——ruminate in silence. The dogs——(*brief bark*)—— are hushed and the hens——(*brief cackle*)——sprawl torpid in the dust. We are alone. There is no one to ask.

Lest we forget the artificial nature of the work, lest we be too easily lulled into a 'poetic' mood, this gently elegiac speech *must* be destroyed to some extent. Beckett, I am sure, feels that no sugar but hides a pill, no dreamy voice but veils a harshness or an emptiness. So other voices (of 'nature') deny the postulate that no one is there, just as the 'soliloquy' of Hamm is technically destroyed by the presence of the listening Clov.

What *All That Fall* gives us is a dramatic poem, compounded from two different kinds of radio play, moving in its comic and ragged pathos in a twist of irony to a shattering conclusion. The birthday of Dan is the deathday of a child and a hen; all move in the same direction and all struggle with the unchanging condition of man in language which to both Dan and Maddy is a 'dead language'.

Well, you, know, it will be dead in time, just like our own poor dear Gaelic, there is that to be said.

Urgent baa.   (p. 35)

In this kind of world where deliquescence, decay and violent, sudden death are the 'events' so movingly presented, what response could the play elicit from its protagonists to the preacher's text for the following day?

'The Lord upholdeth all that fall and raiseth up all those that be bowed down.' (*Silence. They join in wild laughter. They move on. Wind and rain.*

Dragging feet, etc.) Hold me tighter, Dan! (*Pause.*) Oh. yes!

(p. 39)

And with this little uplift into a moribund's tenderness we are ready to be hit by the play's end.

Embers

As a radio play *Embers* is quite different from its predecessor. The radio out of which the sounds and voices come is both the vehicle for the sounds and also an old man's head. The reality of the voices and the situation is problematic. The sound of the sea is of special significance to the protagonist, as the sight of the sea is to Stephen Dedalus in the opening of *Ulysses*, and, as there is no other person's presence to give any guarantee that we have a fictional seaside as a setting for a fictional voice, we may certainly doubt the 'reality' of it all. Ada's voice is remote throughout and she makes no noise on the shingle. Her conversation with Henry oscillates between the past shared with Henry and Addie and the present shared in Henry's imagination.

Henry is old, and the radio-drama is in his head. The sea has haunted him and the noise of its movement fills his ears. He has expedients to distract himself from the present, time past and time future, and his story. The time past is not simply constant but something that can be and has been used up. His father will no longer respond to his calling; Ada is in process of being used up:

> *Ada:* I suppose you have worn him out. (*Pause.*) You wore him out living and now you are wearing him out dead. (*Pause.*) The time comes when one cannot speak to you any more. (*Pause.*) The time will come when no one will speak to you at all, not even complete strangers. (*Pause.*) You will be quite alone, with your voice, there will be no other voice in the world but yours. (pp. 32–3)

Henry carries his people about like gramophone records which he can play, and the past though almost part of a mechanical memory is precarious. It can be summoned, but not as readily as stage-directions. When Henry wants a particular sound, horse's hooves or a drip or a door's slam, he can have it or reject it at will, but human voices from the past are not so easily available. There is even a sense in which consolation has a serial quality moving from Ada, who has been brought back from the dead past, to his father who once could be brought back but who no longer answers the invocations, to Christ, the most distant and unrecallable of all:

> Ada! (*Pause.*) Father! (*Pause.*) Christ! (*Pause.*) (p. 36)

When all else fails the mind of Henry is thrown back on itself and its story. We are unsure of the status of the story, as the two old men, Holloway the doctor and Bolton who summons him, may well be a means of Henry's presenting his own difficulties to himself. Holloway is mentioned by Ada to Henry as a doctor whom he might consult (or might have consulted, if the voice of Ada can only comment on past events):

> There's something wrong with your brain, you ought to see Holloway, he's still alive, isn't he? (p. 30)

So, the story, which by definition (if Henry is Bolton) is unendable, can only elaborate the past experiences of Henry with his father, and his present and past awareness of a deep trouble. The voice can spend itself on setting the scene, in elaborating the details as a novelist would, but can never come to the revelation from Bolton which would express in words what is inexpressible. The story can stand for the situation as a metaphor, and the creative imagination can use its energies in fiction but can never do more than create a metaphor.

So, we see Henry and the sea, Henry and the past, Henry and his story. All that remains is time future. And there lies emptiness. Consulting his diary at the end of the play, we hear that there's nothing for this evening, nothing for Friday but the plumber at nine, nothing on Saturday, and nothing on Sunday:

Nothing, all day nothing. (*Pause.*) All day all night nothing. (*Pause.*) Not a Sound.

Sea.   (p. 36)

We end with no human sound, but the constant sound of the sea. The sea as the infinity symbol, as the place of his father's death and unrecovered body, the place of the love of Henry and Ada, is the metaphor for the dereliction of a man haunted by time, isolated and facing loneliness now and an empty future, constantly aware of death.

The story with its 'embers', and its world made strange in snow, is a story which belongs to a *Dubliners* collection; truncated, foreshortened, well known, rehearsed and magically special, it is, in the end, 'no good'. Presumably it is 'no good' because the fictional old men, Bolton and Holloway, become too real:

that's it, that was always it, night, and the embers cold, and the glim shaking in your old fist, anyway, Please! Please! (*Pause.*) Begging. (*Pause.*) Of the poor. (*Pause.*) (p. 36)

The sliding into 'your old fist' makes the status of the speech ambivalent. We are unsure about Henry, as he may well be remembering his father's imploring him to go for a swim with him the day he drowned, and so guilt is involved (*The Agenbyte of Inwyt*) or Henry is Holloway, Henry becoming Holloway as his father becomes Bolton. It is Holloway who has the last response in the story, who covers his face against the look in Bolton's eyes:

Holds it high again, naughty world, fixes Holloway, eyes drowned, won't ask again, just the look, Holloway covers his face, not a sound, white world, bitter cold, ghastly scene, old men, great trouble, no good. (*Pause.*) No good. (ibid.)

The play with its compression, and with the privacy of a mind opened up for us, as the radio becomes the head of the speaker, has its own beauty and its own realm of rich suggestion. We have focussed more and more sharply the isolation and the coming 'Deserts of vast Eternity' as the time runs on and the man has to face 'not a sound', nothing to distract him from himself.

Cascando

Cascando presents us with a variation on the Voice telling its story, the one it hopes will be the last, but being partnered willy-nilly by Music, both being 'opened' and 'closed' by another, a superior. The superior has no Voice, yet can approve of the way the story goes but can never find anything other than images in his world. Voice pants on desperately in anxiety trying to get his story to catch up 'the other', in this case Woburn. All names are significant, and as this is the only name, what significance in a name 'Woe-burn'; what significance in the sea, the leaving of land and the launching into the sea for the island? As much and as little as one likes: 'An image, like any other'.

Yet the Opener can open the doors of both Voice and Music. He has no answers left to the old questions, and to have a Voice which tells the same stories, the stories which hopefully lend to the one story, which, hopefully, can be ended, is the one asset that Opener has. The creative artist is a caged beast, murmuring in the dark incessantly, and his story which he is not conscious of is being judged, opened, approved of. The Opener has therefore a double function, that akin to the external stimulus or light or bell, and also that of the detached part of the mind which is not the story-Voice, not the creative or obsessionally mad Voice.

Of course, the story nears its end: if the Voice can catch up with the man and witness his death one knows the end will be complete, but all the Voice can do is end on an impotent note of urging itself on.

'Come on . . . come on——

Silence'   (p. 48)

Both Woburn and the Voice are in travail. Both are urging each other on, now more at the end of their tether, deeper into the degradation. Opener believes in the reality of his creatures, but we are made aware that no one else would: 'All is mental.'

They say, He opens nothing, he has nothing to open, it's in his head. They don't see me, they don't see what I do, they don't see what I have, and they say, He opens nothing, he has nothing to open, it's in his head. I don't protest any more, I don't say any more, There is nothing in my head.

I don't answer any more.
I open and close.   (p. 43)

Another time and we would see that the emptied artist, locked in his isolation-ward, taken as mad by others, is Beckett's last word. The artist has been reduced to this desolation of emptiness, of ever repetitive and unendable stories, and the radio becomes the head empty but full.

Henry's head is the *mise en scène* for the play *Embers*, and this time there is no name, only the image-name Woburn, a figurative fiction. The image which controls this play is less theatrical than mechanical— adjacent doors of a mental ward being opened and closed by an authoritarian warder no longer the creator only the controller. The model for Opener might be that of a man twiddling the knobs of a radio. From programme to programme.

The reduction from *Embers* has become bleaker. There is no comedy, no rhetorical relief, no sense of artistic generosity. We have only the barest schematisation, itself rich in imagistic suggestion, but bared down, pared down. We are in the world of the enigmatic narrator of *The Unnamable*:

. . . I deny nothing, I admit nothing, I say what I hear, I hear what I say, I don't know, one or the other, or both, that makes three possibilities, pick your fancy, all these stories about travellers, these stories about paralytics, all are mine, I must be extremely old, or it's memory playing tricks, if only I knew if I've lived, if I live, if I'll live, that would simplify everything, impossible to find out. . . . (p. 416–17)

Eh Joe

In this short television piece Beckett has explored the nature of the play where the camera becomes an active participant in the drama and neither the recorder of events (the analogue of the omniscient author's shifting and controlling point of view) nor Orson Welles's idea that 'the camera must be the eye of the director, it must record his feelings'.

Joe hides himself away from all eyes, from all sources of intrusion, and the doors of all openings must be locked and covered with hangings, and this means, absurdly, even the cupboard door. We are made to observe these acts of desperation by walking behind Joe. We only recognise this when we realise that each of Joe's movements is seen from behind, and we take some time to realise that what we accept now, naturally, in the presence of the seeing eye of the camera (which is the audience's view on the scene) is being identified with the present but unheard Voice. Joe's mind cannot be isolated in the way that he obviously hopes that he, as a body, can. No matter how many bars, shutters or blankets he hides behind, the enemy is already unseen but present.

Joe is a lonely and ageing man, intent on becoming emptied of others, emptying them from his memory as best he can, and he is a parody of St Joan. He has voices which speak to him, but not voices of consolation or power, but voices which haunt, taunt and paralyse. The voices which have already been stilled are those of his parents and 'Others . . . All the others . . . Such love he got . . . God knows why . . . Pitying love . . . None to touch it . . . And look at him now . . . Throttling the dead in his head'. The trouble is that this voice claims a status which is quite different from that of all the other voices of the past. This insinuates that it does not come from his head as did the others and, therefore, cannot be stifled or murdered in the way the others have been. And what it has to tell is the suicide of a girl engaged to Joe whom Joe had treated badly, cavalierly. Joe has his belief in God, 'your Lord', and has a knowledge, therefore, of the four last things 'Death, Judgment, Hell and Heaven'. The Voice can taunt Joe, in accordance with this established belief for Joe, with God's voice 'Thou fool thy soul' ('This night thy soul is required of thee') and 'Mind thou art' ('Remember Man that thou art dust and unto dust thou shalt return'). If the torment of conscience, of having been the cause of a young girl's suicide, isn't hell enough, then the Voice makes it plain that this is only a 'penny farthing hell you call your mind'. The rackety old machine ('huddled in dirt the reasoning engine lies') is nothing compared with the real thing, which obviously waits for Joe.

Meanwhile the little hell goes on and refuses to be stilled. The poetic celebration of the girl implicit in the truncated narration is complexly presented. The details of the girl's death are verified, circumstantial, but are those of the imagination. The girl's attempts at death were unwitnessed and the Voice takes on an ambivalent status, part Recording Angel, part the imagination of Joe which rehearses the scenes constantly.

The girl who 'dies for Joe':
'Taking Joe with her . . . light gone . . . *"Joe Joe"* . . .'

is ironically poised by the Voice against Christ who 'died for Joe' as He died for everyone:

'*There's love for you* . . . Isn't it, Joe? . . . Wasn't it, Joe? . . . *Eh, Joe?* . . . Wouldn't you say? . . . Compared to us . . . Compared to Him . . . *Eh. Joe?*

She: Us: Him: 'us' is the relationship which was that of a couple who no longer love each other, and the Voice had left Joe for someone 'Preferable in all respects . . .', so that the past relationship can be the reason why the Voice can be concerned, as an ex-wife might be concerned for an ex-husband, but can also be the basis for a continuing hatred, a spiteful and bitter taunting. Joe has been a pig, and has driven the Voice away to find 'a better', and he has been the cause of suicide in another, but this 'Voice' we need to remember is a curiously compounded 'Voice'. It contains in itself the essence of 'Feminine Love', all those who have been wife or lover have a common Voice which is external to Joe, as mother and father are not, and we can see that 'I' and 'she' are both integrated into 'Voice'. Both 'I' and 'she' are seen terminally, at the end of the affair, with 'the best's to come'. Now Joe is seen terminally with the ends of his affairs troubling his mind, and 'the worst's to come' when all Voices are finally stilled, when all the portals onto the past miseries are closed, when he will have achieved the perfect stasis of the 'Silence of the grave without the maggots'. Then *He* will start 'in on you . . . When you're done with yourself . . . If ever you are'.

This is not a play about conscience, but of hallucination, but this hallucination is not simply explicable in terms of imagination. It is explicable only in terms of realities which are above or beyond the ordinary realities. A man's mind is his Hell, but there is always worse to come. Where we have aspired to the condition of silence (as Joe has become silent in himself—*De nobis ipsis silemus* as the Unnamable puts it) and then one by one silenced the voices that haunt us, which trickle in our mind, there is always the worse to come.

Again, nothing can end, even though we are dealing in ends and fragments. The horror is that of the surviving mind. If we have opted out of the world of distractions from reality, of work, of play, of people, and have come closer to the condition of the mystic or Irish monastic, then we approach not peace or contentment in a Thomas

Merton *Waters of Silence* manner of abnegation but the condition of terror. The mind goes on, but the man decays at the top, like Swift.

Poetry remains ironically embedded in this work, jagged slivers of a once whole beautiful narration whose purpose is not any more to entrance, to move, but to cut and pain:

> Step clinging the way wet silk will . . .
> Moon going off the shore behind the hill . . .
> Stands a bit looking at the beaten silver . . .
> Scoops a little cup for her face in the stones . . .

Joe once had a 'powerful grasp of language', and this remains in fragments. It had once been at the service of seduction and celebration; now it turns in on him as torment, taunt and threat.

The nine movements of the camera into maximum close-up must be seen as related to a special meaning. The fourth, or intermediate position, is the position for Voice, the wife's voice say, to have her say. She 'started in' on Joe when she was strong and she tells Joe what Joe knows about the whole business of voices in the head, the nearness to stifling of this Voice, and the imagination which may make the Voice unending, unendable. This would seem to be the final position for this Voice, to achieve.

The ninth movement is the longest and here we have the final version for this evening of the Voice. But this time Voice 1 moves into Voice 2, not simply by assuming another personality, but assuming a different role. This is the worst of all for Joe, the place of his fractured poetry, his 'powerful grasp of language' which now grasps his mind so powerfully. It is also the parody of the consoling stories which other Beckett characters tell themselves, getting close to an end. This is an end which constantly returns, and Gabriel Conroy has become transformed to 'Poor old Joe'. There is the final irony of recognition:

> Gone are the days
> When my heart was young and gay;
> Gone are my friends
> From the cotton fields away;
> I hear their gentle voices calling
> Poor Old Joe.
> I'm coming, I'm coming,
> Though my head is bending low.

A 'coon song' sobs its way behind the drama and the camera's eye is cold, unemotional, with no director's emotion. All emotions are combined into the cold terror and anguish of a man trapped in a world of anguish and near to death which is no consolation, simply an entrance into an eternal confrontation of the miseries other people's deaths seem to have released him from here in life.

Happy Days

First performed in 1961 in New York, this two-act play presents the audience with a double problem. What is the situation and what does it mean? Winnie exists in a mound topped by scorched grass and she is being stimulated into wakefulness by a bell, and she mentions the bell for sleep, though we never hear that. Time is abolished and has been replaced by an unchanging light, an empty landscape and an arbitrary division into wakefulness and sleep to replace day and night.

Winnie has to fill the 'time' and she does this by performing trivial feminine tasks either 'to keep herself nice', like paring her finger nails, or randomly selecting objects from her capacious handbag. Talk fills her time, though she is aware that she must not use up her small resources of words and things too quickly. She must be careful, and dole out her succedanea in small units.

What now? (*Pause.*) Words fail, there are times when even they fail. (*Turning a little towards WILLIE.*) Is that not so, Willie? (*Pause. Turning a little further.*) Is that not so, Willie, that even words fail at times? (*Pause. Back front.*) What is one to do then, until they come again? Brush and comb the hair, if it has not been done, or if there is some doubt, trim the nails if they are in need of trimming, these things tide one over. (p. 20)

Her 'days' are apparently endless and only slightly variable. Willie's occasional responses to her questions, occasional 'tit bits from *Reynolds' News'*, his activities with handkerchief or in crawling backwards down into his hole are those which have gone on, with slight variations and changes, for a long 'time'. Her 'day' begins with prayer and is to end with prayer (which we do not hear and so may not have been prayed). 'World without end Amen' (p. 10), the ending of the *Gloria*, is both the indication of this unending but downward descending purgatory and the central irony of the 'Happy Days': 'Glory be to the Father, and to the Son, and to the Holy Ghost. As it was in the beginning, is now, and ever shall be, World without end Amen.'

But there is not here the simple eternal instant of no time, but the characteristic downward curve of man's life. The second act is obviously closely related to the first: Winnie still has her hat on at the beginning of the act, her bag and parasol are where they were, and the revolver is still 'conspicuous to her right on mound'. But things have altered. This act is very short and the bell is more insistent that the eyes do not close. In the beginning of the first act Winnie was allowed to close her eyes and pray, but immediately she does close her eyes in the second act the bell shrills her into opening them immediately and will keep on insisting on 'eyes open'. So no prayer. Willie too has few responses, no little appearances, no little movements to distract or involve her, until his final epiphany 'dressed to kill'. Then we see him fully for the first time, and his dress suggests his wedding day. Gone is the boater with the club ribbon, now replaced by a full morning suit, but his age has not receded back to that far day. He is weak and can only manage on all fours, can only murmur 'Win' twice, and cannot succeed in scrambling up the mound to his wife. He cannot touch her, kiss or kill her. This last ironic epiphany must mean the end of love, the return to its beginning-ending, the impossibility of any more tit-bits from *Reynolds' News*, always the same; 'always' has changed to 'never'. The third act must be silence, the burial of the head up to the eyes, no mouth to talk, no one to talk to, only the mind to think, to be made to think.

The second act, as in *Waiting for Godot*, is another scene from the infinite series of 'days', to use the only word we have, but taken from the 'sweet old style' when there were days, taken from nearer to the end of the infinite series, but not the end.

The pathetic life of a woman changes to a stronger charged irony as she sees only too clearly the miserable pretence at love from Willie that she had been content, perforce, to live with for a whole married lifetime. The trivia are taken away from her as she is more and more engulfed in the mound, and she is thrown increasingly on inner resources that are equally trivial, but her little all. She is courageous in facing her lot; she has no alternative but to face it and her chance of using Brownie to escape from the living hell has receded into the far past of another day. But she can tell herself her story and she can sing her song. Her story is enigmatic and frightening, of little Mildred/Millie and the mouse running up her thigh until it was too late, despite the screams, for anyone to help her. I suppose that the story isn't one of a simple recall kind, though, as always with Beckett's character's stories, one sees fact and fiction being woven together. If this mouse-experience has been Winnie's, then the power of the story is that of obsession;

if not, then it is a substitute or metaphor for some terror which she cannot articulate or put into words. Whatever it is, she can now tell it, or she has now no alternative but to tell it, as she cannot rummage in her handbag for distractions. The story does not make her face any reality but gets her one degree closer to emptying herself, of bringing her all up, as she says in the first act.

The song is that of the musical box which she can no longer play. She can sing of love, the dance and touching finger tips now that she can no longer even sway to the music as she could in the first act; nor give or receive love. Nor can Willie reach her. She is not allowed to drift off into either fantasy or sentimental reminiscence as she is in Act I:

My first ball! (*Long pause.*) My first ball! (*Long pause. Closes eyes.*) My first kiss! (*Pause. WILLIE turns page, WINNIE opens eyes.*) (p. 15)

Now, having ended her sentimental song with 'It's true, it's true,/You love me so!' the stage directions are *Pause. Happy expression off. She closes her eyes. Bell rings loudly. She opens her eyes.* etc.

4

BREATH-CLOCK BREATH:

How It Is

When *The Unnamable* was completed and the fictional road had become an impasse to Beckett, it became increasingly clear that the only way of going on was to rehearse the old tune, to do a little better what had already been done. But Beckett did find a way, a new departure combining the voice speaking and the effort involved in speaking, a rhythmic organisation of breathed words caught by the reader's eye and ear. The reader becomes a new Dante whose ears catch a version of those sighs which Virgil describes in Canto VII of *Hell* as belonging to those whose anger has damned them:

> This too for certain know, that underneath
> The water dwells a multitude, whose sighs
> Into these bubbles make the surface heave,
> As thine eye tells thee wheresoe'er it turn.
> Fix'd in the slime, they say: 'Sad once were we,
> 'In the sweet air made gladsome by the sun,
> 'Carrying a foul and lazy mist within:
> 'Now in these murky settlings are we sad.'
> Such dolorous strain they gurgle in their throats,
> But word distinct can utter none.
>
> (Cary's translation)

Comment C'est was the way out from the *ne plus ultra* of *The Unnamable* and it appeared in 1961, and as *How It Is* in 1964. This novel subsumes *The Unnamable* and orders the torrent of words without punctuation by introducing a measure of parsimony which tightens and increases the power of the work. It is organised into three parts on the simplest of models (before, during and after), a total account of an experience, its penurious plenitude. The difficulty is that there is no truth, not a word of truth, in it, and there is no one to accept the responsibility for the fiction, to give anything more satisfactory as a reason for its being written at all than the necessity of something being said, some explanation for 'how it is'. That's how life is—denuded of meaning with a voice which must, for reasons unknowable, find what it conceives to be reasons for things being as they are. Out of the experience of the human need for human, of the need and desire to learn, to instruct, to be solaced by story, memory, of filling the emptiness that is the centreless person, to love and be loved, to feel the warmth of another human person by one's side, arises this given life, the life granted 'this time' to the voice of the fictional creation. This fictional creation is, like all the later Beckett voices, autonomous and insufficient, hampered and living off scraps and fragments of a mind, remnants of a generous liberal education now wasting into ruin and dereliction. It has made for itself not 'a pillow of words' this time but the prisoner's 'oakum' to be unpicked with sore fingers and bleeding thumbs to make rope: 'oakum of old words ill-heard ill-murmured'. A voice murmurs, its words toneless and without the differentiation that any punctuation would give, then silence. The effect seen on the page is of a prose-poem, but the ear becomes accustomed to the breath-stabs of words panted out by the voice which, *ab initio*, repudiates responsibility for the whole work by its words:

how it was I quote before Pim with Pim after Pim how it is three parts I say it as I hear it. (p. 1)

The model for human life of the journey towards the other, the sojourn with him and then the abandonment, of the long tale of a life, of all lives, is one part of the novel's function. Within that function the metaphor operates of someone who has fallen to the very bottom of existence, fallen through from a life 'up there in the light' down to the mud, where, solitary and doomed to a prostrate position, he drags himself forward laboriously yard by yard in the mud, in the dark, in a straight line from west to east (ironic counter-journey to life's metaphor of sunrise to sunset) towards Pim.

Anxious to have done with the telling, the voice rushes ahead at times summarising its lesson, retroverting to times past, engaging in brief retrospective flashes of life 'up there in the light'. These flashes may be invention, may be memory, their only real function being other than enlightenment. They are hiccups of time, brief, convulsive, and the images are objectified, sparse in emotion. The natural scenery is more emotionally lively and beautiful than the human beings submerged in it. The setting is 'poetic': 'to crown all glorious weather egg-blue sky and scamper of little clouds', and the returning image of the landscape carries the beauty of a forgotten Ireland:

We are if I may believe the colours that deck the emerald grass if I may believe then we are old dream of flowers and seasons we are in April or in May and certain accessories if I may believe them white rails a grandstand colour of old rose we are on a racecourse in April or May. (p. 32)

This has the quality of a kind of snapshot turned up in a drawer, vivid and sharp in detail yet objective. What 'I' have in my hand is 'an undefinable object' as something forgotten yet vaguely shown on the photograph, then seen later as 'a little pale grey brick', and the voice is not remembering simply; it is re-creating, questioning and trying to see. The voice is not exacting the sweet pathos of an idyllic but long-dead time; this is obviously the danger which makes it important to treat the human as mechanistically as possible, to treat the young lovers to a good dose of savage description, to knock the sweetness out of it all:

seen full face the girl is less hideous it's not with her I am concerned me pale staring hair red pudding face with pimples protruding belly gaping fly spindle legs sagging knocking at the knees wide astraddle for greater stability feet splayed one hundred and thirty degrees fatuous half-smile to posterior horizon figuring the morn of life green tweeds yellow boots all those colours cowslip or suchlike in the buttonhole. (p. 33)

And the fatuity of the love-exchange is measured by the mechanism of the eating and swallowing and avowing:

Suddenly we are eating sandwiches alternate bites I mine she hers and exchanging endearments my sweet girl I bite she swallows my sweet boy she bites I swallow we don't yet coo with our bills full (ibid.)

my darling girl I bite she swallows my darling boy she bites I swallow brief black and there we are again dwindling again across the pastures hand in hand arms swinging heads high towards the heights smaller and smaller out of sight first the dog then us the scene is shut of us (p. 34)

The sequences are those of the cinema, and the finale, after interruption of blackness and a return to the mud, is like a couple advancing towards the camera and appearing to move through it into the unseeable space behind the camera:

it is dusk we are going tired home I see only the naked parts the solitary faces raised to the east the pale swaying of mingled hands tired and slow we toil up towards me and vanish

the arms in the middle go through me and part of the bodies shades through a shade the scene is empty in the mud the sky goes out the ashes darken no world left for me now but mine very pretty only not like that it doesn't happen like that   (p.35)

The cinematographic model seems important. As at the ending of a simple tale of bucolic love with the young innocents moving, happily and tired, out of a day of beauty and simplicity in the mountains into an evening beyond the day, one might well say: 'Very pretty! Only not like that. It doesn't happen like that.' This would be a way of acknowledging an image, artistically foreshortened, of life's grace and beauty, which is certainly aesthetically pleasing or amusing, but which the saddened heart knows is an insufficient statement about life. Romance is for romances. To treat one's memory in this way is to acknowledge that it is an artistic invention, that its 'reality' is not of the same order as a 'memory'. We are in the same arena of memory as that fought in Krapp. But, in the end, what 'I' have done is to fill some of the interminable time in which 'I' am plunged.

Of course 'I' cannot tell his fiction in sequence, cannot organise his story into its three parts without confusing and conflating. The second part is present in the first, the irruption of Pim into before-Pim is in-excusable and something is wrong. Pim's buttocks, which are one of the important sources of communication between the voiceless tormentor who needs the voice of the tormented to speak, are brought in by association in Part I. 'I' sees himself as an object in a landscape of mud and darkness, an object created by the artist-creator out of himself to give comfort to a comfortless existence:

How often kneeling how often from behind kneeling from every angle from behind in every posture if he wasn't me he was always the same cold comfort

one buttock twice too big, the other twice too small unless an optical delusion here when you shit it's the mind that wipes I haven't touched them for an eternity in other words the ratio four to one I always loved arithmetic it has paid me back in full

Pim's though undersized were iso he could have done with a third I fleshed them indistinctly something wrong there but first have done with my

travelling days part one before Pim how it was leaving only part two leaving
only part three and last

(p. 41)

'Something wrong there.' What is wrong would seem to be not so
much the curious reflection that Pim could have done with a third
buttock, presumably to bring the quality of total flesh up to some
imagined standard, but the incautious admission that Pim is 'my'
creation ('I fleshed them indistinctly'). Also that, though Pim has not
yet been created in terms of the story, he already has an existence that
is irrevocable. This is a twice-told tale, at least. We are on a circuit
which 'I' have passed before, and some kind of penance is being enacted by 'I', whose tale has to be told again and again. So the 'this time'
which one is so conscious of in Part I takes on a real meaning.

'I always loved arithmetic it has paid me back in full.' Indeed, the
whole model for *Comment C'est* is of an arithmetical even-handed
'justice'. To invent the other towards whom I journey is to have to
invent some other who will be in need of me. To have less would be an
offence against justice, the system of needing and needed would be
incomplete. Therefore there must be another who will make me speak,
make me respond to his stimuli for communication, for solace, for
entertainment, for information. But to posit this tripartite system which
is the nearest parodic approach to the Three Persons of the Trinity is
logically insufficient. For justice endlessly to be satisfied there must be
an infinite series of pursued and pursuing.

'I' always has to find words to fill the time of waking. When the
prayer for sleep doesn't work more words must be found 'and they all
spent'. And now is introduced the potential or real 'witness' of all this
struggle and impotent effort. To assume 'esse est percipi' is to assume
a witness of one's existence in order that it be guaranteed, but, as in
Film, the observer is a terrible fiction who turns out to be oneself
observing oneself. Here the fiction may be real, may be another way of
turning words to the advantage of filling the void, the vacuity, the
inanity.

he would need good eyes the witness if there were a witness good eyes a
good lamp he would have them the witness the good eyes the good lamp
(p. 50)

But if there were a witness he would not simply be the guarantor of the
reality of the existence of the 'I', he would have to report on the be-

haviour and actions of 'I' (for reasons unknown). This parody of the recording angel is important as partly involving the whole theological parody of Beckettian fiction and also as another idea to be exploited when it will serve a need. The Joycean epiphany of the Ballast Office clock in *Stephen Hero* comes simply back as deflated to its function of telling the time:

This triviality made him think of collecting many such moments together in a book of epiphanies. By an epiphany he meant a sudden spiritual manifestation, whether in the vulgarity of speech or of gesture or in a memorable phase of the mind itself. He believed that it was for the man of letters to record these epiphanies with extreme care, seeing that they themselves are the most delicate and evanescent of moments. He told Cranly that the clock of the Ballast Office was capable of an epiphany. Cranly questioned the inscrutable dial of the Ballast Office with his no less inscrutable countenance. —Yes, said Stephen. I will pass it time after time, allude to it, refer to it, catch a glimpse of it. It is only an item in the catalogue of Dublin's street furniture. Then all at once I see it and I know at once what it is: epiphany. (*Stephen Hero*, Ed. Theodore Spencer, Four Square Books, 1966, pp. 215–16.)

Back from revelation to the furniture of Dublin:

to the scribe sitting aloof he'd announce midnight no two in the morning three in the morning Ballast Office brief movements of the lower face no sound it's my words cause them it's they cause my words it's one or the other I'll fall asleep within humanity again just barely (p. 50)

And sleep comes with a further dead image of a schoolboy's fable revelation. Back from the furniture of Dublin to a beautiful but entirely false epiphany:

and there a beautiful youth meet a beautiful youth with golden goatee clad in an alb wake up in a sweat and have met Jesus in a dream (ibid.)

Hope is abandoned and a gleam of hope remains. The paradox remains. Man is not alone in his misery. There is a procession of us and this is our only comfort:

what comfort in adversity others what others those dragging on in front those dragging on behind whose lot has been whose lot will be what your lot is endless cortège of sacks burst in the interest of all (p. 53)

Man is sustained by his indifferent environment where needs are satisfied unpalatably but really, where the dead past vomits itself up for the mind to chew on, where there are both tins and tin opener, which, when they are used up or all lost, will be the sign of the end of life. But the mind cannot really be brought to end its metaphor, to explode the image, to die. Whether it wants to or not there is always a further extension of the metaphor possible against all the odds. So when, neatly enough in some ways, the mind has allowed its provision sack, its sustainer, comforter, pillow and companion-surrogate, to become worn out, abraded, then it is not the end it should have been; something will turn up to spoil it all:

no emotion all is lost the bottom burst the wet the dragging the rubbing the hugging the ages old coal-sack five stone six stone that hangs together all gone the tins the opener an opener and no tins I'm spared that this time tins and no opener I won't have had that in my life this time

so many other things too so often imagined never named never could useful necessary beautiful to the feel all I was given present formulation such ancient things all gone but the cord a burst sack a cord I say it as I hear it murmur it to the mud old sack old cord you remain

(p. 51)

Hamm's ending is like this. Though his whole universe has run out, 'old stauncher you remain'; one thing remains to give some small solace, to hold on to as you pass hopefully into oblivion. All is frustrated by Clov's remaining on the threshold of departure—all unfortunately frustrated, that's how it is. In this present case there are alternatives, the one being absurdly impossible, the other impossibly absurd: either God's miraculous intervention or the encounter with Pim, both intrusions into the locked world of the self:

Or a celestial tin miraculous sardines sent down by God at the news of my mishap wherewith to spew him out another week

... the hand dips clawing for the take instead of the familiar shine an arse two cries one mute end of part one before Pim that's how it was before Pim

(pp. 53-4)

Pim, the essential victim, tortured into communication, is none the less the creature

who but for me he would never Pim we're talking of Pim never be but for me anything but a dumb limp hump flat for ever in the mud but I'll quicken him you wait and see and how I can efface myself behind my creature when the fit takes me now my nails (p. 58)

'I' is a parodic God creating Man in his own image, fashioning and modelling a companion, an artistic artefact:

I hoist myself if I may say so a little forward to feel the skull it's bald no
delete the face it's preferable mass of hairs all white to the feel that clinches
it he's a little old man we're two little old men something wrong there (p. 60)

'I' changes his mind about many aspects of his creation while he is
creating. We know, for example, from Part I, that Pim has a watch
(p. 44, 'to have Pim's timepiece something wrong there . . .') but when
'I' comes to discover it he finds first a 'watch wristlet' and then changes
his mind to 'a big ordinary watch complete with heavy chain' which
Pim holds tight in his fist. Where a normal author would have deleted
or decided, we are given, as ever in this late fiction, a process of com-
position which highlights the untruth of the events being recounted as
real. Its usefulness as an item in the total account is very limited and
rapidly ended:

from it to me now part three from way off out on the right in the mind to me
abandoned the distant ticking I desire no more profit from it none whatever
no more pleasure count no more the unforgiving seconds measure no more
durations and frequencies take my pulse no more ninety ninety-five it keeps
company that's all it's ticking now and then but break it throw it away let it
run down and stop no something stops me it stops I shake my arm it starts
no more about this watch (pp. 65–6)

Different stories conflate here. The one story of my being left in the
course of time abandoned by Pim to await my tormentor Bom, and
hearing the gradual disappearance of the departing Pim by the lessen-
ing tick of the watch, is followed immediately by that of another time
when mine is the watch, when time is strapped to my arm, which I
would willingly dispose of but am prevented by 'something'. Obviously, perhaps, the watch was always 'mine' but attributed to Pim, and
that real time is not only inexorable but infinite, 'vast tract of time'.
The horror of time is emptied of the bravura of 'What a Misfortune'
where the unfortunate Belacqua Shuah is informed by his fiancée that
she has brought him 'the grandfather and mother of a period clock':

He turned his face to the wall, He who of late years and with the consent of
Lucy would not tolerate a chronometer of any kind in the house, for whom
the local publication of the hours was six of the best on the brain every hour,
and even the sun's shadow a torment, now to have this time-fuse deafen the
rest of his days. It was enough to make him break off the engagement. (pp.
139–40, *More Pricks than Kicks*)

But concern with chronometers in this void is just another of the many
'extravagances', needless accumulations of 'facts', 'observations' and

so on which are all meaningless because superfoetatory, superarroga-
tion pure and compound. To complicate matters for the narrator, the
other's sack is not burst. Now, either all burst or none burst for there
to be even-handed justice. So, even here in the mud, inequity exists,
the inequity of God's love that passes human understanding:

not burst Pim's sack not burst there's no justice or else just one of those
things that pass understanding there are some

older than mine and not burst perhaps better quality jute and with that still
half-full or else something that escapes me sacks that void and burst others
never is it possible the old business of grace in this sewer why want us all
alike some vanish others never

(p. 68)

This time the couple will be 'Pim', next time there will be a couple,
'Bom', with roles reversed of tormentor-tormented:

the one I'm waiting for oh not that I believe in him I say it as I hear it he can
give me another it will be my first Bom he can call me Bom for more com-
modity that would appeal to me m at the end and one syllable the rest
indifferent (p. 67)

It's all one. Memories of the life above demanded by Pim will be
demanded by Bom.

I talk like him Bom will talk me only one kind of talk here one after another
the voice said so it talks like us the voice of us all quaqua on all sides then
in us when the panting stops bits and scraps that's where we get it our old
talk each his own way each his needs the best he can it stops ours starts starts
again no knowing (p. 84)

So Pim's memories of the love and the death of love and the loved one's
suicide or accidental death are both circumstantial and vague, both a
symbolic universal statement of human weakness and the inevitable
decay in the business of living, and the possible memory of a single
individual. The pathos and the brilliant clarity of detail of colour in
this murky absence of light here in the mind are very striking, though
qualified by the eccentricities of voice imported by the narrator
('. . . the flowers I held them at arm's length before her eyes that was
my visit and she forgiving marguerites from the Latin pearl they were
all I would find . . .', p. 85). And all this, the characters, the emotions
of the dead past, the two ancients glued together, murmurer and
hearer, are too much to be borne, too excruciating to be suffered. Yet
they must be suffered:

E

did he think did we think just enough to speak enough to hear not even
comma a mouth an ear sly old pair glued together take away the rest put
them in a jar there to end if it has an end the monologue (p. 87)

This would be Hamm again, cruelly demanding that Nagg and Nell
be 'bottled' and anxious only for his own monologue, except that
Hamm himself, the monologuist, is rejected:

But nothing of the kind is possible
dream then that at last certainly not me dream me Pim Bom to be me
    think pah   (ibid.)

But who or what he is the speaker cannot know; whether anything was
ever said by anyone to anyone, whether all is internal, whether all is
fictional, no knowing. Confusion, 'great confusion no knowing'. The
terror lies in the very fiction itself, having to pursue the metaphor
once it has started, having to have Bom, having to become the victim-
tormentor as well as the tormentor-victim. There is no having the rose
without the canker, the Blakean invisible worm is necessary to the
rose:

Bom never came if only that but then how end the hand dipping clawing for
the tin the arse instead of the familiar slime all imagination and all the rest
this voice its promises its solaces all imagination dear bud dear worm (p. 88)

The terror of isolation 'all alone there is left all alone alas' creates the
need of the witness and the scribe. Imagination creates Kram the
witness and Krim the scribe in an infinite series of witnesses and
scribes, and, because they inhabit this purgatorial world too, they
have to suffer the tedium of witnessing and reporting on the inactivity
and the murmurs of the solitary who invents a world peopled with tormentors and victims. The circle closes in infinite circularity: a voice
murmuring creating a world of observers who note the murmurs
which are the substance of the fictional work. All is tedium, all delusion, all a vain attempt to 'pass the time', and the observer Kram needs
to keep busy with so little of note to note that he says 'if nothing I
invent must keep busy otherwise death'. But all is denied by the voice,
all reduced to nothing, the scaffolding of the fiction thrown back into
the mud:

that's enough end of extracts yes or no yes or no witness no scribe all alone
and yet I hear it murmur it all alone in the dark the mud and yet (p. 92)

So on into flashes of memory, those common to Bim (victor-tormen-
tor) of life above in the light, of Pam and the death of love, of a loved

dog run over by a dray; into other metaphors of search for asylum, rest and death, the search by sea for an isle; then the need to end, to bring the second part with Pim to an end. E is scored deep, 'then good and deep', followed by more reflections, more scraps from some life or other, then scored again. Painfully N is scored, but the D is never inflicted. The long ending is changed into questionings of Pim, violently attempting to discover the mode of his life down here in the mud, desperately wanting love (though the obscenity negates the potential tenderness of the question 'DO YOU LOVE ME CUNT') and only dredging up the meaningless anguish of life unendable and without meaning or purpose:

if he talks to himself no thinks no believes in God yes every day no wishes to die yes but doesn't expect to no expects to stay where he is yes flat as a cowclap on his belly yes in the mud yes without motion yes without thought yes eternally yes (p. 107)

But Pim can affirm nothing, is sure of nothing, and 'I' am eternally alone.

Part III has to invent again the essential objects of the metaphor, has to struggle to find, then capture in words the body, the sack:

a sack bravo colour of mud in the mud quick say a sack colour of its surroundings having assumed it always had it it's one or the other seek no further ...

a body what matter say a body see a body all the rear white originally some slight spots still say grey of hair growing still that's enough a head say a head say you've seen a head all that all the possible a sack with food a body entire alive still yes living stop panting let it stop ten seconds fifteen seconds hear this breath token of life hear it said say you hear it good pant on

(p. 113–14)

But, as Part III is the sessile state of waiting for Bom, there is nothing to do except think. And thinking is the subject matter of Part III. This means investigating the arithmetic of justice, of puzzling over the logistic problem provided by the fact that the one who journeys leaves his sack behind with the one who remains, and has therefore to pick up a sack of provisions *en route* for his victim. This involves the puzzle of how an infinite number of sacks is to be provided for an infinite series of tormentors and victims, which, absurdly enough, leads to the conclusion of the existence of

an intelligence somewhere a love who all along the track at the right places according as we need them deposits our sacks (p. 150)

But all this depends upon *our* sense of justice, our sense that there must be both victim-tormentor and tormentor-victim, that any series, say fifty million, is insufficient for the needs of the first and last in the series, for they would be either 'deprived of tormentor as number one' would be or deprived of victim as number 50,000,000. Problems of the computation of the speed of progress, of whether communication is possible outside the closed series of any three victim-tormentor-victim (Bem – Pim – Bom) at all compose a mathematical solace. All are hypothetical, self-inflicted problems, and all fall within the statement in Part I, now enacted painfully for us, 'I always loved arithmetic it has paid me back in full', and justifies Ludovic Janvier's quotation from Lautréamont: 'O mathématiques saintes, puissiez-vous, par votre commerce perpétuel, consoler le reste de mes jours de la méchanceté de l'homme et de l'injustice du Grand-Tout'. But, as ever,

all these calculations yes explanations yes the whole story from beginning to end yes completely false yes (p. 158)

These arithmetic calculations, the series of numbers, the figures, show signs in Part III of giving place to a condensed geometry moving internally away from the luminous infinity of series of numbers, the metaphoric geometry of *Imagination Dead Imagine*:

the voice quaqua on all sides then within in the little vault empty closed eight planes bone white if there were a light a tiny flame all would be white ten words fifteen words like a fume of sighs when the panting stops then the storm the breath token of life part three and last it must be nearly ended (p. 140)

Furthermore, the work is noted as being incomplete, as only three parts are given of the four part cycle, where the fourth part would show 'instead of me sticking the opener into Pim's arse Bom sticking it into mine'. But the voice says that Parts II and IV would be indistinguishable, and no apology to the reader is necessary:

loathing most understandable if it be kindly considered that the two solitudes that of the journey and that of the abandon differ appreciably and consequently merit separate treatment whereas the two couples that in which I figure in the north as tormentor and that in which I figure in the south as victim compose the same spectacle exactly (p. 143)

But Part III ends with Part IV's ending. We recognise the similar tormenting questions which end Part II in the ending of Part III. Bom has arrived, though

in the familiar form of questions I am said to ask myself and answers I am said to give myself however unlikely that may appear last scraps very last when the panting stops last murmurs very last however unlikely that may appear (p. 157)

Under the torment of the questions which can have no articulated answer, there can be only screams of pain, though the whole fiction can be denied and turned back into the void:

so things may change no answer end no answer I may choke no answer sink no answer sully the mud no more no answer the dark no answer trouble the peace no more no answer DIE screams I MAY DIE screams I SHALL DIE screams good

good good end at last of part three and last that's how it was end of quotation after Pim how it is

(p. 160)

The whole retroverted fable is a quotation, the denied affirmation is someone else's tale, told by an idiot, but the voice is left in suspension, in isolation between victim and tormentor, in purgatorial and infinite suffering of self.

FARRAGO OF SILENCE AND WORDS:

SHORT FICTION

Because Beckett turned to the short story as a possible way out of his fictional dilemmas after his writing of *Watt*, they have some interest for the critical reader. But when Beckett's fictional creations have become more and more compressed, they take on a very real interest. The more concentrated the style and the shorter the piece, the more and more it approaches a complexly working poem. The sparer the technique the more resonant the fiction, and Beckett has the power to create hauntingly powerful images which reflect on many of our culturally inherited ones. The tautness of the short fictions is Beckett's real achievement.

Short stories

Immediately succeeding the writing of *Watt* and after a novel in French which remained unpublished until 1970 (*Mercier et Camier*), Beckett wrote three stories (and a short story similarly unpublished until 1970, *Premier Amour*) in 1945–6 which he later published as *Nouvelles* with *Textes Pour Rien* in 1954. These were later translated and published in English in 1967 as *The Expelled, The Calmative* and *The End*.

   In these stories we hear, for the first time, the narrator speaking his own story, spinning the words of the story out of himself. The stories represent the life of a man when he is thrown out into the world, without purpose, without orientation and with diminishing means. He is, as it were, born into the cold comfort of the world outside the

room-womb and spends his fading efforts in finding the ideal combination of isolation, self-sufficiency, abnegation of need and desire,
a closed safe place and death. Each of the three stages, the expulsion,
the inexplicable gift of the unknown calmative from a suddenly appearing stranger, and the final expulsion from the hospital or St John
of God's hospice into death gives a kind of unity to the life, but the
ending of the stories in a fictitious narration of the death by drowning,
and by using the calmative set in the past, arouses not only the suggestion that the voice we hear is a dead voice, but also that it is a lying
voice, the fabricator of stories who narrates what never was:

The sea, the sky, the mountains and the islands closed in and crushed me in
a mighty systole, then scattered to the uttermost confines of space. The
memory came faint and cold of the story I might have told, a story in the
likeness of my life, I mean without the courage to end or the strength to go
on. (p. 67)

But the story of the end has been assimilated, before it is told, into a
vision:

Enough, enough, the next thing I was having visions, I who never did,
except sometimes in my sleep, who never had, real visions, I'd remember,
except perhaps as a child, my myth will have it so. I knew they were visions
because it was night and I was alone in my boat. What else could they have
been? So I was in my boat and gliding on the waters. (p. 65)

The story gathers momentum and verisimilitude with details which
constantly make the fictitious reality the more credible, making dis-
coveries about itself, finding its own defining facts and oddnesses:

I got up from my seat in the stern and a great clanking was heard. That was
the chain. One end was fastened to the bow and the other round my waist.
I must have pierced a hole beforehand in the floorboards, for there I was
down on my knees prying out the plug with my knife. The hole was small
and the water rose slowly. It would take a good half hour, everything included, barring accidents. Back now in the stern-sheets, my legs stretched
out, my back well propped against the sack stuffed with grass I used as a
cushion, I swallowed my calmative. (p. 67)

The memories of boyhood are interwoven with the vision and, as in
dreams, contribute to the vision, partly controlling and partly distort-
ing, but they are only of the same order of credibility as the story, and
the *calmative* of the second story is swallowed here in the vision which
ends the third. That was claimed to be real by the fiction, but how far
does the swallowing of the calmative take place in a vision? Does the
vision (proleptic by nature) incorporate the wishes of the present, or

how far does the telling of what is claimed as vision depend upon the incorporation and re-shaping of memory? Does memory or vision matter when all are being placed in the same ambivalence of being told in a dead voice which should perhaps have shaped a different story anyway, which is a story already told somewhere because it is a 'memory', and so did have some existence (as did the life whose story it might have been)?

We see Beckett struggling here with the ideas of man's impossible ending, of fiction and its impossible truth, of a single voice which meticulously tells a story spun out of itself, a story of doubtful validity in itself and of undoubted fiction anyway, when this is not autobiography but Beckett's creation. The stories are memories told in the past and the recognition that what we have been exposed to or treated with are memories of the dead, notes from the underground, and yet not memories but stories which are arbitrary only because the narrator chose them and chose to let them tell themselves:

When I am abroad in the morning I go to meet the sun, and in the evening, when I am abroad, I follow it, till I am down among the dead. I don't know why I told this story. I could just as well have told another. Perhaps some other time I'll be able to tell another, living souls, you will see how alike they are. ('The Expelled', p. 24)

In the second story, we discover that the voice speaks out of an icy bed not knowing when 'I' died and is going to tell 'myself' 'another story, to try and calm myself, and it's there I feel I'll be old, old, even older than the day I fell, calling for help, and it came'. Though dead he lives in terror, though dead he can tell stories, and still needs to tell stories which will, like the calmative of the title, deaden pain. This would satisfactorily reduce the level of sensitivity which could be raised again, unfortunately, by a good night's nightmare and a tin of sardines (p. 36), but the stories, as stories, will be self-cancelling, will have said nothing. 'All I say cancels out, I'll have said nothing' (p. 26).

And there's no point in saying that the past tense indicates a passed time. No time passes except the time of the telling, nothing happened despite all claims to the contrary; all is fiction:

For what I tell this evening is passing this evening, at this passing hour. I'm no longer with three assassins, in this bed of terror, but in my distant refuge, my hands twined together, my head bowed, weak, breathless, calm, free, and older than I'll have ever been, if my calculations are correct. I'll tell my story in the past none the less, as though it were a myth, or an old fable, for this evening I need another age, that age to become another age in which I become what I was. (p. 26)

This evening (time 1) I need another age (time 2), that age to become another age (time 3) in which I became what I was (time 4). Yet 'I' chose 'another story' in which 'I' will be older than 'the day, the night, when the sky with all its lights fell upon me', and this must be the end, *The End*, and this story must be a story about the unreal time between death and the present eternal time after death. But how can I become what I was in this time scale? The (time 1) present evening must be the last in the series of times past and the second story (time 2) is needed for the third story to exist (time 3) in which I became what I used to be 'up there in the light'.

The writer needs to be able to reach an end, a satisfying end to his life, satisfying at least in the telling. He needs to be able to be defined as refuse, as totally peripheral to mankind and society, to become isolated and complete in his self which can then be quietly discarded, 'scattered to the uttermost confines of space'. This process then involves the final expulsion from a temporary asylum which had grown into the habitual sessile life, institutionalised:

I saw the familiar objects, companions of so many bearable hours. The stool, for example, dearest of all. The long afternoons together, waiting for it to be time for bed. At times I felt its wooden life invade me, till I myself became a piece of old wood. There was even a hole for my cyst. (pp. 44–5)

He is turned out into a world which is beyond his categories of comprehension, which is at variance with his inner world. The denuded poetry of his natural observations accommodates all things without emotional involvement. The human is seen objectively, inhumanly:

Now I was making my way through the garden. There was that strange light which follows a day of persistent rain, when the sun comes out and the sky clears too late to be of any use. The earth makes a sound as of sighs and the last drops fall from the emptied cloudless sky. A small boy, stretching out his hands and looking up at the blue sky, asked his mother how such a thing was possible. Fuck off, she said. I suddenly remembered I had not thought of asking Mr Weir for a piece of bread. (p. 46)

The city is half-remembered, seems strange and mostly altered, and he is afflicted with a longing for asylum:

I longed to be under cover again, in an empty place, close and warm, with artificial light, an oil lamp for choice, with a pink shade for preference. From time to time someone would come to make sure I was all right and needed nothing. It was long since I had longed for anything and the effect on me was horrible. (p. 48)

He is cheated by his landlady out of most of his money—a good stroke to push him towards the end—and is now reduced to penury. Here his last real contact with human society occurs when he meets a man from the past who lived in a cave by the sea, owning an ass which was old and small yet just big enough to transport 'sand, sea-wrack and shells to the townsfolk, for their gardens'. He lives with this man with the ass who shows the sort of kindness the speaker has led us to believe he wants. He has quiet and a roof over his head; for the admired paraffin lamp is substituted the regular flashing of a lighthouse, and the man with the ass offers to fulfil the longing:

If I preferred to be alone he would gladly prepare another cave for me further on. He would bring me food every day and drop in from time to time to make sure I was all right and needed nothing. (p. 55)

The rejection of the offer is, in one sense, the rejection of the longing, and it is important to notice the identity of the habitual details of the invented lodgings—there is always the same model of a room, daily visited and supplied with a tray of food and a chamber-pot. We are being helped to the fantasies of a man used to hospice, used to the routine, the occasional visit to make sure all is right and his lodging with the Greek or Turkish (?) woman is compounded from this basic memory:

About noon she brought me a big tray of food and took away the tray of the previous day. At the same time she brought me a clean chamber-pot. The chamber-pot had a large handle which she slipped over her arm so that both hands were free to carry the tray. The rest of the day I saw no more of her except sometimes when she peeped in to make sure nothing had happened to me. (pp. 49–50)

From a temporary sojourn in an unutterably sordid cabin in the mountains, he is dragged into life by a cow which he tries to milk, and having reached the city again, is forced to beg for his living. This he does with impotent delicacy and clumsy adroitness responding to his recognition of the habits of those willing to give charity. 'What they like above all is to sight the wretch from afar, get ready their penny, drop it in their stride and hear the God bless you dying away in the distance.' He wears his old tutor's dark glasses, the one who had given him the *Ethics* of

Arnold Geulincx, and graduates from a tin hanging from a button of his coat, to a large tin on the pavement, to a 'kind of board or tray and tied it to my neck and waist'.

So, on the fringe of man's society, he holds on to life, but has no political response (which might have come from a disaffected reject) for the fragments of a speech from a rabble-rousing Marxist which impinge on his failing senses. He has no interest in being seen as the victim of a capitalist society and only wants oblivion and to have done with it all; he has nothing to cheer him, needs no hopes, no objectives. The political speech is reduced to

Union ... brothers ... Marx ... capital ... bread and butter ... love. It was all Greek to me. . . . Then he bent forward and took me to task. I had perfected my board. It now consisted of two boards hinged together, which enabled me, when my work was done, to fold it and carry it under my arm. I liked doing little odd jobs. So I took off the rag, pocketed the few coins I had earned, untied the board, folded it and put it under my arm. Do you hear me, you crucified bastard! cried the orator. Then I went away, although it was still light. But generally speaking it was a quiet corner, busy but not overcrowded, thriving and well-frequented. He must have been a religious fanatic, I could find no other explanation. Perhaps he was an escaped lunatic. He had a nice face, a little on the red side. (pp. 61–2)

He is well on his way towards the end lying in the boat which he found in a shed on the riverside, a grandiose living ship-burial where he awaits his end. He is retreating into the private self as distinct from that which he calls 'a being outside of me', having become 'more independent of recent years':

Then no one came any more, that no one could come any more to ask me if I was all right and needed nothing, distressed me then but little. I was all right, yes, quite so, and the fear of getting worse was less with me. As for my needs, they had dwindled as it were to my dimensions and become, if I may say so, of so exquisite a quality as to exclude all thought of succour. To know I had a being, however faint and false, outside of me, had once the power to stir my heart. (p. 64)

This ancient moribund, safe from the rats in his land-locked ship, launches into his vision of drifting downriver out into the open sea and, chained to the boat's bow, he eases out the plug from a hole in the floorboards. There, back against the sack stuffed with grass which he used as a cushion, he dies (in his vision). To tell the real life is impossible, because in reality there is neither courage to end nor the strength to go on.

Swift's Gulliver, that misanthropist, has changed to the cold-eyed Beckett's Man. He sees our world through eyes less bitter than Swift's, less of an obvious or dramatic *saeva indignatio*, but none the less witnesses the ugliness, cruelty and despicable reality we bourgeois like neither to witness nor record. The cabin in the mountains is credible but unpleasant, and we have this to reckon with if we would be more than self-deluded seekers after the aesthetically pleasing or picturesque. Love has been committed here:

What he called his cabin in the mountains was a sort of wooden shed. The door had been removed, for firewood, or for some other purpose. The glass had disappeared from the windows. The roof had fallen in at several places. The interior was divided, by the remains of a partition, into two unequal parts. If there had been any furniture it was gone. The vilest acts had been committed on the ground and against the walls. The floor was strewn with excrements, both human and animal, with condoms and vomit. In a cowpad a heart had been traced, pierced by an arrow. And yet there was nothing to attract tourists. I noticed the remains of abandoned nosegays. They had been greedily gathered, carried for miles, then thrown away, because they were cumbersone or already withered. This was the dwelling to which I had been offered the key. (p. 56)

Texts for Nothing

Since then [1950] I haven't written anything. Or at least nothing that has seemed to me valid. The French work brought me to the point where I felt that I was saying the same thing over and over again. For some authors writing gets easier the more they write. For me it gets more and more difficult. For me the area of possibilities gets smaller and smaller. . . . In the last book—'L'Innommable'—there's complete disintegration. No 'I', no 'have', no 'being'. No nominative, no accusative, no verb. There's no way to go on.
     The very last thing I wrote—'Textes pour rien'—was an attempt to get out of the attitude of disintegration, but it failed. (Israel Shenker, 'Moody Man of Letters', *New York Times*, CV, Sunday 6 May 1956, section 2, pp. 1 and 3.)

Controlled by the sense of disintegration which *The Unnamable* had for him, Beckett tried, and failed, with *Texts for Nothing*, to control the chaos. John Fletcher in *The Novels of Samuel Beckett* (London 1964, p. 196) and Eugene Webb in *Samuel Beckett* (London 1970, p. 154) suggest that we read *'texte pour rien'* as an analogy for *'mesure pour rien'*, the musical term for a bar's rest. So, Webb persuades us,

a bar's rest in music is a very special sort of silence, it is silence not just silence in an absolute or simple sense, it is silence as an integral part of a formal structure. Music is something which, in itself, means nothing, but which nevertheless embodies beauty. As Beckett has found himself more and more restricted in his thematic material, he has become increasingly concerned with form. . . . (p. 154)

Beckett certainly intended his work to have a formal musical relationship, but exactly how is not quite clear. It is true that we are being encouraged to see the thirteen 'texts' as organised into 12+coda, as text XIII asks if it can finish off the sequence:

But what more is it waiting for now, when there's no doubt left, no choice left, to stick a sock in its death-rattle, yet another locution. To have rounded off its cock-and-bullshit in a coda worthy of the rest? Last everlasting questions, infant languors in the end sheets, last images, end of dream, of being past, passing and to be, end of lie. (p. 135)

But one sees that text XIII, as 'coda', is only one of the multiple ironic possibilities present in this passage. The voice speaking, like the voice of *The Unnamable*, is unsure of its status, unsure of its existence, and aware of a voice impotent yet going on. It wants nothing yet it speaks, and the despair of the narrator is that it will never end, but aware that there may be some formal requirement needed to round out, to round off, the work. But to have rounded off 'cock-and-bullshit' is no great achievement, especially when, allusions pressing in on the literary narrator as they always do, we are made aware of the 'cock-and-bull' story of the unended *Tristram Shandy*. And, again, the whole set of terms used for ending are subsumed under 'locution', just a way of speaking. 'In a manner of speaking' takes on an ironic smile when the whole work is concerned with the manner of artistic speaking when there's behind it Beckett's own acknowledged manner of working:

I'm working with impotence, ignorance. I don't think impotence has been exploited in the past. (Shenker, 'Moody Man of Letters', p. 3.)

The 'infant languors' in these 'end sheets' is the combination of the desire to get himself born, the lassitude of the old man on his death's bed, and the writer's knowledge of words existing on numbered sheets. It sums up the whole exercise of the *Texts for Nothing*, of confronting the unconfrontable which underlies all the literary characters of Beckettian fiction, and of having to write without the possibility of creation. If there seems the possibility that 'I' will have been transposed to a condition beyond humanity, a condition of Yeats's soul in 'Sailing to Byzantium' for example, then this must be shown as a 'locution', a 'lie'. Where Yeats sees himself 'out of nature' as a golden bird, set on a golden bough to sing

> To lords and ladies of Byzantium
> Of what is past, or passing, or to come . . .

this is mocked by Beckett as that condition of art which aspires to the changeless, to the permanently significant.

The *Texts for Nothing* are thirteen central written thoughts usable for a set of discourses 'on nothing'. They are, by definition, incomplete, and their relationship can only be in their coherence in a single, embracing subject (here 'Nothing', on the analogy of 'Charity' or 'Religious Hope').

The 'texts' are all attempts made in 'evenings' to find a way out of a dead world, attempts by the narrator to find himself, to come alive. But all attempts are futile because, while a voice goes on interminably and then cuts off, and faint glimmerings of hopeless hope are continually being granted so that the possibility of knowing something certain will come 'tomorrow', still nothing is known and the voice goes on:

And were there one day to be here, where there are no days, which is no place, born of the impossible voice the unmakable being, and a gleam of light, still all would be silent and empty and dark, as now, as soon now, when all will be ended, all said, it says, it murmurs. (XIII, pp. 135–6)

So the work ends, but it cannot be said to conclude. The formal ending is mirrored on that of *The Unnamable* and prefigures that of *How It Is* in that the voice goes on, is not stilled for ever, as it should be in a perfect fiction, aesthetically and structurally an artistic whole. Beckett severs the connection between the formal structure and the thematic content, allowing us to recognise musical structure and then to qualify that recognition for us by making us uneasy and troubled rather than soothed and pleased by an object of great formal beauty.

The Texts go over most of the themes of *The Unnamable*, and the narrator sometimes blames others for his condition; in IV he accuses the 'same old stranger as ever, for whom alone accusative I exist' of trying to make him exist when he does not exist:

When he had me, when he was me, he couldn't get rid of me quick enough, I didn't exist, he couldn't have that, that was no kind of life, of course I didn't exist, any more than he did, of course it was no kind of life, now he has it, his kind of life, let him lose it, if he wants to be in peace, with a bit of luck.

His life, what a mine, what a life, he can't have that, you can't fool him, ergo it's not him, what a thought, treat him like that, like a vulgar Molloy, a common Malone, those mere mortals, happy mortals, have a heart, land him in that shit, who never stirred, who is none but me, all things considered, and what things, and how considered, he has only to keep out of it. (no. IV, p. 88)

But it is seen that the struggle with the other is an inner struggle against treating 'the stranger' as a 'vulgar Molloy, a common Malone, those mere mortals'. This would serve him right, but it represents a kind of writing no longer possible, a world of fiction now in the far past and irrecoverable. 'I' am no longer there:

for the moment I'm not there, nor anywhere else what is more, neither as head, nor as voice, nor as testicle, what a shame. . . . (no. XI, p. 124)

But, even so, the invention of 'I' can proceed through images which can only be invention, not the remembering of a real past, and the invention of the lonely moribund in pain nearing the final dissolution is the whole life-story *in vitrio*. 'I' can appear 'just when most needed, like the square root of minus one' (p. 124), necessary but impossible, and the 'I' is created young-old, 'a snotty old nipper' in an ancient body, its functions painful and ceasing, both a wished-for and a loathed humanity, and at the very verge of that humanity, the awareness of a pain and desperation in the face of life and the human:

as old as the world and no less hideous, amputated on all sides, erect on my trusty stumps, bursting with old piss, old prayers, old lessons, soul, mind and carcass finishing neck and neck, not to mention the gobchucks, too painful to mention, sobs made mucus, hawked up from the heart, now I have a heart, now I'm complete, apart from a few extremities, having terminated their humanities, then their career, and with that not in the least pretentious, making no demands, rent with ejaculations, Jesus, Jesus. (p. 125)

But no invention is credible enough to deceive the narrator into discovering himself, and even the stratagem of sneaking up with 'those who knew me' ('it's as though I were among them') won't work. Either the voice watches 'I' approach, then recede 'shaking my head and saying, Is it really he, can it possibly be he?', or the voice is 'alone where I am',

. . . alone where I am, between two parting dreams, knowing none, known of none, that finally is what I had to say, that is all I can have had to say, this evening. (p. 127)

The section ends on the puzzled ambiguity of 'had to say', the task to perform and the only possible expression: the 'pensum' and the poverty.

Every section builds up the 'others'; every section has its 'homeless mes and untenanted hims' (XII, p. 130) and we cannot talk of a single narrator, only of an endless stream of talk with no *one* talking, yet always *one* talking. We must talk rather of the absences, the denials of presences, the failure to create either a personality or a credible situation, and agree with the forlorn hope of the 'knowing non-exister' that it is a

blessing it's all down the drain, nothing ever as much as begun, nothing ever but nothing and never, nothing ever but lifeless words. (p. 131)

The final coda, section XIII, sums up the poignancy and emptiness of the desire of the creative artist to make an impression, to create something which will have some permanence, by echoing the antiphon in *Waiting for Godot*:

Estragon: All the dead voices.
Vladimir: They make a noise like wings.
Estragon: Like leaves.
Vladimir: Like sand.
Estragon: Like leaves.
   Silence.   (p. 62)

The dying voice here 'wants to leave a trace ,

yes, like air leaves among the leaves, among the grass, among the sand, it's with that it would make a life, but soon it will be the end, it won't be long now, there won't be any life, there won't have been any life, there will be silence, the air quite settled that trembled once an instant, the tiny flurry of dust quite settled. (XIII, p. 133)

Rather than the furious monologue with all the impotent frustration of the Unnamable's terminus, rather than the terror of 'all these words', this time there is a calm and gentle conclusion. The anguish is not suppressed but presented as silence, that special silence not of the bar's rest, but

the screaming silence of no's knife in yes's wound. (XIII, p. 135)

The constant denial of affirmations, the no-knowledge of the non-exister, is not a cool absence of the terrors of life, but an even more terrifying world where murder is committed by no on yes and where the voice must vainly murmur on in its struggle to articulate something, to leave even a trace.

In the end we agree with Beckett that he fails to progress much beyond *The Unnamable*, but we see more clearly that, while his concern with formal structure becomes more insistent, formal structure for its own sake will never be a sufficient end in itself. There must be the separation of form as seen in the old sense of shape and structure, from form in a new sense of that which promises shapely structure, but which denies that promise by using the shape as something to terminate, arbitrarily, an activity which is seen to be interminable.

Compressed fiction

During the last few years since the writing of *How It Is* the fiction has become extremely short, only a few pages, and has approached the condition of silence, of ending, more and more closely. All the work has been composed in French and all has been translated into English by Beckett himself, the single exception being the tiny *Dans le cylindre* (*Biblio.*, XXXV, no 1, January 1967) which remains untranslated.

Each of these works has its own interest and each tackles the situation of the static or nearly static condition of the dying mind, and most of these works (so a publishers' note to their English versions in *No's Knife* tells us) are *residua*, all that remain of longer works. So one can see that Beckett has been trying more and more to write fiction and managing less and less. The task of creation has become nearly impossible, and the published remnants suggest exactly why.

Imagination Dead Imagine presents the puzzle clearly enough in its title (perhaps even more clearly in the original French, *Imagination Morte Imaginez*) inviting us to imagine a dead imagination. The substance of the fiction is an image of a dome within which are two naked bodies back to back and head to toe in foetal positions. But nothing happens. There is no 'event' for any fictional interest. The real interest is that this final image created by a near-dead imagination is so richly suggestive, a poetic image compounded of geometry ('Two diameters at right angles AB CD divide the white ground into two semicircles ACB BDA') and the human skull's resemblance to the dead world of the moon (as in *Malone Dies*) and to the dome of Shelley.

This last shudder of the imagination before it expires and has to live with 'no trace anywhere of life' leaves the narrator with all the potentiality of his brain-couple coming alive out of their womb-tomb of a skull completely unfulfilled. For human involvement we have substituted for us almost totally mechanical images, and yet the impression given by the narrator is one of an effort to present accurately and carefully an imagined situation, as though what was imagined came like a dream or vision in which he had no control and yet over which only he has control. The world is subject to heat and light, cold and dark, and there is no knowing whether the imaged world will continue into infinity with the same alternation, or whether it will be stilled in either the light or the dark. The Imagination, now that it is expiring under its last engagement with itself, must lose the image, but the loss will be sad and nothing like the thankful emptying of the mystic:

Leave them there, sweating and icy, there is better elsewhere. No, life ends and no, there is nothing elsewhere, and no question now of ever finding again that white speck lost in whiteness, to see if they lie still in the stress of that storm, or of a worse storm, or in the black dark for good, or the great whiteness unchanging, and if not what they are doing. (*No's Knife*, p. 164)

The place for both making the image and the place for locating the image has become a cranium, a head minus the rest of the face: no eye-sockets, no nose, no mouth, no ears. Without a world to encounter, without the senses, the dying imagination creates life which can never get born, foetuses which grow old in the cranium's tomb.

Another approach to the obsession of ending and yet having to speak, having to imagine, having to write, is that of *Ping* (published in French as *Bing* in 1966). Here the voice is recorded at its task of creation, but the situation which it is creating is totally static; a naked body in a kind of upright coffin, or cell, or night-watchman's hut, stares ahead. But the voice is too tired, too broken, to have a simple consistency in its telling. It has very few words and constantly repeats this handful of words in varying combinations. It constantly wants to cease its telling, but its task is 'unover' until the final word 'over', and the thirty-three 'Pings' which might seem a kind of punctuation in the work, alongside the formal punctuation of full stops, is the sound of a bell demanding that the impossible task go on. We are used to Beckett's probe or prod operating on dramatic characters in *Act Without Words II*, *Happy Days* and *Play*, and we can recognise the cruelty of these ways of insisting that characters either perform their task, or perform to order when, like Winnie in *Happy Days*, they would prefer to sleep. Here the impersonal little bell controls the narrator but is not simply located outside the narrator as it is in *Happy Days*.

In a simple sense 'Ping' is the author's prod and the author is the cruel God-like taskmaster who tortures the voice into its story-telling. It is as though the narrating voice were creating an image of itself as static, as beyond movement, beyond speech and with only the eyes open. The conclusion is pitiful because those eyes which have been the only colour in the blank white world of the image ('light blue almost white') have been seen as 'imploring' and end as again 'imploring'. The image created by the tortured and defeated imagination itself wants to cease, wants to be released as does its creator.

Light heat all known all white heart breath no sound. Head haught eyes white fixed front old ping last murmur one second perhaps not alone eye unlustrous black and white half closed long lashes imploring ping silence ping over. (*No's Knife*, p. 168)

The effort of making, the impossibility of making, and the torture into making, result in a tattered image, moving in its bleak sadness and its strange poetry of reiteration and poverty.

The separation of the pen that records and the voice that speaks is achieved by a dramatic economy in *Ping* which is an advance over previous fiction, though *Enough* returns to the more literary paradox of the writer being at odds with the recorder. But, whereas the paradoxical impossibility of writing, with nothing to write about and nothing to write with, and yet writing, was pursued throughout *The Unnamable*, *Enough* will only spend an opening paragraph on this business ('the art and craft'). The separation of the voice from the pen and the impossibility of the voice's ever going silent is presented with extreme bareness:

All that goes before forget. Too much at a time is too much. That gives the pen time to note. I don't see it but I hear it there behind me. Such is the silence. When the pen stops I go on. Sometimes it refuses. When it refuses I go on. Too much silence is too much. Or it's my voice too weak at times. The one that comes out of me. So much for the art and craft. (*No's Knife*, p. 153)

In a much simpler mode than either of the other two residual pieces of *Imagination Dead Imagine* and *Ping*, we hear the lonely voice in *Enough* of a woman 'entering night' remembering her wandering life with an old man whom she left. From him she learnt everything:

All I know comes from him. I won't repeat this apropos of all my bits of
knowledge. The art of combining is not my fault. It's a curse from above. For
the rest I would suggest not guilty. (*No's Knife*, p. 154)

But her story is so barren of events that we are aware that it is an impossible fabrication, an invention to comfort the isolation of a human
person, an invention to calm the terrors of lonely death. Though it
seems to have the kind of details which makes for verisimilitude, we
know just what the trilogy has to say about that, and we come to see
just what inventions are necessary to sustain the futile emptiness and
horror of life. Truth for the fiction is a special kind of lie:

We lived on flowers. So much for sustenance. He halted and without having
to stoop caught up a handful of petals. Then moved munching on. They had
on the whole a calming action. We were on the whole calm. More and more.
All was. This notion of calm comes from him. Without him I would not
have had it. Now I'll wipe out everything but the flowers. No more rain. No
more mounds. Nothing but the two of us dragging through the flowers.
Enough my old breasts feel his old hands. (ibid., p. 159)

'Too much silence is too much', so the narrator needs a little something, enough. She needs just enough to help her create something to
hold on to, a 'pillow of old words' like Watt, or the sustaining final
'memories' of Krapp.

A whole world of possibilities for an invented life is scaled down to
a wandering with an old man bent double who 'was not given to talk.
An average of a hundred words per day and night. Spaced out. A bare
million in all.' All the misery of intense human experience is expunged
and the aim is to create a 'calmative', a fictional anaesthetic.

Coda: The Rest is Silence

The path has been followed relentlessly towards silence, and we too
follow this route, observing a richly gifted comic genius depositing his
riches, sloughing off his learning, a latter-day *Peregrinus*, the wandering Irish scholar, who is emptying himself of himself.

This pilgrim's regress has the quality of a seriously honest confronting of the anguish of life, of the individual and of the world. It holds
out no hope and yet its bleakness cannot in any simple sense be
charged with being depressing. Though you cannot go on you go on.

His moribunds have passed into common currency as 'Beckett's
bums'; but from this literature of failed people, rejects or derelicts,
failed writers, a whole world of hopelessness and emptiness, he has

created a vision of the world as hell which has spoken to people of their own condition.

Recognition and reward have come late. A Nobel Prize is one thing but his increasing readership is another.

CHRONOLOGY

1906 (Born Foxrock, Co. Dublin)

1929 'Dante . . . Bruno . . . Vico . . . Joyce' in *Our Examination Round His Factification for Incamination of Work in Progress*: Shakespeare & Co, Paris 1929; reissued Faber and Faber, London 1936 and 1961.

1930 *Whoroscope*: Paris 1930; collected in *Poems in English*, Calder, London 1961.

1931 *Proust*: Chatto and Windus, London 1931; Calder, London 1958; London 1965 (with *Three Dialogues*).

1934 *More Pricks than Kicks*: Chatto and Windus, London 1934; Calder, London 1970.

1935 *Echo's Bones and Other Precipitates*: Europa Press, Paris 1935; collected in *Poems in English*, 1961.

1938 *Murphy*: Routledge, London 1938; Calder, London 1963.

1951 *Molloy*: Editions de Minuit, Paris 1951.

1951 *Malone Meurt*: Editions de Minuit, Paris 1951.

1952 *En Attendant Godot*: Editions de Minuit, Paris 1952.

1953 *L'Innommable*: Editions de Minuit, Paris 1953.

1953 *Watt*: Olympia Press, Paris 1953 and 1958; Grove Press, New York 1959; Calder, London 1963.

1954 *Waiting for Godot*: Grove Press, New York 1954; Faber and Faber, London 1956.

1955 *Nouvelles et Textes pour Rien*: Editions de Minuit, Paris 1955.

1955 *Molloy* (translated into English by Patrick Bowles in collaboration with the author): Olympia Press, Paris 1955; Grove Press, New York 1955; collected into one volume with *Malone Dies* and *The Unnamable* in 1959 in Paris (Olympia Press), New York (Grove Press) and London (Calder).

1956 *Malone Dies*: Grove Press, New York 1956; Calder, London 1958.

1957 *Fin de Partie* and *Acte sans paroles* in one volume: Editions de Minuit, Paris 1957.

1957 *All that Fall*: Faber and Faber, London 1957.

1957 'From an Abandoned Work': *Evergreen Review*, I, no. 1, 1957; reprinted by Faber and Faber, London 1958; collected in *No's Knife*, Calder and Boyars, 1967.

1958 *The Unnamable*: Grove Press, New York 1958; collected into one volume with *Molloy* and *Malone Dies* in 1959.

1958 *Endgame* and *Act without Words* in one volume: Faber and Faber, London 1958.

1958 'Krapp's Last Tape': *Evergreen Review*, II, no. 5, 1958; published with *Embers* by Faber and Faber, 1959.

1959 'Embers': *Evergreen Review*, III, no. 10, November–December 1959.

1960 *Bram van Velde* (translated into English by the author and Olive Classe): Grove Press, New York 1960.

1961 *Comment c'est*: Editions de Minuit, Paris 1961.

1961 *How It Is*: Grove Press, New York 1961; Faber and Faber, London 1964.

1961 *Happy Days*: Grove Press, New York 1961; Faber and Faber, London 1962.

1962 'Words and Music': *Evergreen Review*, IV, no. 27, November–December 1962; published with *Cʒacando* and *Play* by Faber and Faber, 1964.

1963 'Cascando': *Evergreen Review*, VII, no. 30, 1963.

1964 *Play*: Faber and Faber, London 1964.

1965 *Imagination morte imagineʒ*: Editions de Minuit, Paris 1965.

1965 *Imagination Dead Imagine*: Calder and Boyars, London 1965.

1966 *Asseʒ*: Editions de Minuit, Paris 1966.

1966 *Bing*: Editions de Minuit, Paris 1966.

1967 'Dans le cylindre': *Biblio*, XXXV, no. 1, January 1967.

1967 'Ping': *Harper's Baʒaar*, no. 3067, June 1967.

1967 *Stories and Texts for Nothing* (all translated by the author except 'The Expelled' and 'The End' which were translated by Richard Seaver in collaboration with the author): Grove Press, New York 1967.

1967 *No's Knife* (a collection of short fiction: 'The Expelled', 'The Calmative', 'The End', 'Texts for Nothing', 'From an Abandoned Work', 'Enough', 'Imagination Dead Imagine', 'Ping'): Calder and Boyars, London 1967.

1967 *Come and Go: A Dramaticule*: Calder and Boyars, London 1967.

1967 *Eh Joe*: Faber and Faber, London 1967.

1969 *Sans*: Editions de Minuit, Paris 1969.

1970 *More Pricks than Kicks*: Calder and Boyars, London 1970.

1970 *Mercier et Camier*: eventually published Editions de Minuit, Paris 1970.

1970 *Lessness*: Calder and Boyars, London 1970.

BIBLIOGRAPHY

Entries marked with an asterisk are contained in *Samuel Beckett: A Collection of Critical Essays (Twentieth Century Views)*, Ed. Martin Esslin, 1963

NOVEL CRITICISM

Early Fiction

R. Federman, *Journey into Chaos: Samuel Beckett's Early Fiction*, 1965.
Ruby Cohn, '*Watt* in the Light of *The Castle*', *Comparative Literature*, xiii, Spring 1961. no. 2, pp. 154–66.
W. A. Strauss, 'Dante's Belacqua and Beckett's Tramps', *Comparative Literature*, xi, Winter 1959, no. 1, pp. 250–61.
D. Mintz, 'Beckett's *Murphy*: A "Cartesian" Novel', *Perspective*, 11, Autumn 1959, pp. 156–9.
*Jacqueline Hoeffer, 'Watt', *Perspective*, 11, Autumn 1959, pp. 166–82.
Susan F. Senneff, 'Song and Music in Samuel Beckett's *Watt*', *Modern Fiction Studies*, XI, 2, Summer 1964, pp. 137–49.

Fiction in General

Melvin Friedman, 'The Novels of Samuel Beckett; an amalgam of Joyce and Proust', *Comparative Literature*, XII, no. 1, Winter 1960.
J. Fletcher, *The Novels of Samuel Beckett*, 1964.
E. Webb, *Samuel Beckett: a study of his Novels*, 1970.
*D. Wellershoff, 'Failure of an Attempt at de-mythologization'.
R. Cohn, *Samuel Beckett: The Comic Gamut*, 1962.
J. Cruickshank (Ed.), *The Novelist as Philosopher: studies in French Fiction 1935–60* (essay by Esslin).
M. Robinson, *The Long Sonata of the Dead: A Study of Samuel Beckett*, 1969.

THEATRE

M. Esslin, *The Theatre of the Absurd*, 1964.
J–J. Mayoux, 'The Theatre of Samuel Beckett', *Perspective* 11, no. 3, 1959.
D. Suvin, 'Beckett's Purgatory of the Individual', *Tulane Drama Review*, XI, no. 4, Summer 1967.
*Eva Metman, 'Reflections on Samuel Beckett's Plays'.

L. Pronko, *Avant-Garde: the Experimental Theatre in France*, University of
    California Press, 1962.
J. L. Styan, *The Dark Comedy: The Development of Modern Comic Tragedy*, 1962.
C. Duckworth (Ed.), *En Attendant Godot*, 1966.
L. E. Harvey, 'Art and the Existential in *En Attendant Godot*', *PMLA*, LXXC
    no. 1, March 1960.
J. Fletcher, 'The Arrival of Godot', *MLR*, vol. 64, no. 1, January 1960.
P. Mélèse, *Beckett* (*Théâtre de tous les temps*, no. 2), 1966.

GENERAL STUDIES

H. Kenner, *Samuel Beckett: A Critical Study*, 1962.
R. Cohn, *The Comic Gamut*, 1962.
M. Robinson, *The Long Sonata of the Dead*, 1969.
L. Janvier, *Pour Samuel Beckett*, 1966.
J. Onimus, *Beckett* (*Les Ecrivains devant Dieu*), 1968.
L. Harvey, *Samuel Beckett, Poet and Critic*, 1970.
J. Fletcher, *Samuel Beckett's Art*, 1967 and 1971.

COLLECTIONS OF ESSAYS

M. Friedman (Ed.), *Configuration Critique*, no. 8.
M. Esslin (Ed.), *Samuel Beckett: A Collection of Critical Essays* (*Twentieth Century
    Views*), 1963.
——*Modern Drama*, vol. 9, no. 3, December 1966 (essays on Beckett's theatre;
    a special collection on *Waiting for Godot*; essays on *Endgame, All That Fall,
    Krapp's Last Tape* and *Play*).
J-L. Barrault (Ed.), *Cahiers Renaud-Barrault*, no. 44, October 1963.
——*Endgame: A Collection of Critical Essays* (*Twentieth Century Views*).

BIBLIOGRAPHIES

Good selective bibliographies can be found in:

J. Fletcher, *The Novels of Samuel Beckett*.
M. Robinson, *The Long Sonata of the Dead*.
Ruby Cohn, *The Comic Gamut*.
M. Friedman (Ed.), *Configuration Critique*, no. 8.
E. Webb, *Samuel Beckett, a Study of his Novels*.

INDEX

AESCHYLUS, 90
Aristotle, 92
Augustine, St, 88

BARNARD, G. C., 55–6
Beckett, Samuel:
    Act Without Words II, 144
    All that Fall, 102–8
    Bing, 144
    Breath, 22, 86
    Cascando, 111–12
    Comment C'est, 119–23
    Dans le cylindre, 143
    Eh Joe, 22, 86, 112–16
    Eleutheria, 20, 86
    Embers, 108–11, 112
    En Attendant Godot, 20, 21
    Endgame, 21, 93–100, 108, 125, 128
    Enough, 145–6
    Film, 22, 86, 123
    Fin de Partie, 21, 93, 98
    Happy Days, 22, 116–18, 144, 145
    How It Is, 14, 119–31, 140
    Imagination Dead Imagine, 21, 83, 143–4, 145
    Imagination Morte Imaginez, 143
    Krapp's Last Tape, 14, 100–2, 146

    Lessness, 21
    Malone Dies, 20, 49, 50, 60–71, 76, 78, 85, 96, 143
    Mercier et Camier, 20, 132
    Molloy, 20, 33, 49–60, 61, 65, 66, 71, 73, 80, 89
    More Pricks Than Kicks, 14, 16–18, 126
    Murphy, 18–19, 25–34, 62, 65, 74, 81, 85
    No's Knife, 143–6
    Nouvelles, 20, 21, 132–8
    Ping, 144–5
    Play, 144
    Textes Pour Rien, 20, 21, 132, 138–43
    The Unnamable, 20, 36, 43, 49, 62, 71–85, 92, 112, 119, 138, 139, 140, 142, 143, 145
    Waiting for Godot, 22, 67, 86, 87–92, 93, 117, 142
    Watt, 14, 19–20, 34–48, 62, 63, 65, 66, 91, 92, 97, 132, 146
    Whoroscope, 13
Behan, Brendan, 87
Blake, William, 128
Bunyan, John, 55
Byron, Lord, 90

CARY, REV. HENRY FRANCIS, 17, 119

Clay, Theresa, 100
Coleridge, Samuel Taylor, 69

DANTE, 17, 18, 119
d'Aubarède, Gabriel, 15, 62
Descartes, René, 13, 14, 72–3, 81
Driver, Tom F., 14–15
Duthuit, Georges, 73

ELIOT, T. S., 37, 103

FLETCHER, JOHN, 138
Freud, Sigmund, 96

Genesis, Book of, 93
Georgias, 45
Geulincx, Arnold, 136–7

HOBSON, HAROLD, 88
Hoefer, Jacqueline, 44
Horace, 90

JANVIER, LUDOVIC, 27, 29, 130
Jeremiah, Lamentations of, 95
Joyce, James, 14, 15, 16, 18, 23, 25,
    102, 105, 108, 110, 115, 124
    Anna Livia Plurabelle, 15
    A Portrait of the Artist as a
        Young Man, 102
    Dubliners, 36, 110, 115
    Finnegans Wake, 14, 15
    Our Examination Round the
        Factification for Incamination
        of Work in Progress, 16
    Stephen Hero, 14, 124
    Ulysses, 102, 108

KAFKA, FRANZ, 66
Keaton, Buster, 22

Keats, John, 38
Kenner, Hugh, 41, 88

LAUTRÉAMONT, COMTE DE, 130
Leibniz, 29
Leventhal, A. J., 45, 47

MARX BROTHERS, 27
Mayoux, Jean-Jacques, 42, 43, 86
Merton, Thomas, 115
Murdoch, Iris, 18

PAUL, ST, 47
Proust, Marcel, 14, 102

ROCHESTER, EARL OF, 46
Rothschild, Miriam, 100

SARTRE, JEAN-PAUL, 38
Schneider, Alan, 89
Schubert, Franz, 103
Senneff, Susan Field, 41
Shelley, Percy Bysshe, 143
Shenker, Israel, 138, 139
Spencer, Theodore, 124
Sterne, Laurence, 34, 62, 139
Swift, Jonathan, 46, 116, 138
Synge, John Millington, 104

THOMAS, DYLAN, 18

VAN VELDE, BRAM, 73, 77

WEBB, EUGENE, 138
Welles, Orson, 112
Wordsworth, William, 27, 38

YEATS, W. B., 38, 139–40